40 Days

An account of a discipline

D0911578

Gnostic Press ⚹

Abdullah Dougan

40 Days

An account of a discipline

Published in 1978 by Gnostic Press
3 Addle Hill, Carter Lane, London EC4 V5AY, England.
55 Tramway Road, Birkdale, Auckland 10, New Zealand.

Printed in Hong Kong by Colourcraft Ltd.
Type set in Auckland by Institute Press Ltd.

Dedicated to Rosalie,

the best of women,
for her tolerance of Neil

Acknowledgements

Grateful thanks to Abdul Wheeler for his typing of the handwritten manuscript while on tour, also to Pat Field for her great help with the editing without which this book would never have seen the light of day in this form.

Contents

The beginning

Neil was born on 15th April 1918, at Longburn in New Zealand, to a middle class family. His mother was a third generation New Zealander whose grandfather, a major in the Indian Army, had been sent to New Zealand for the Maori wars. Her mother was half Jewish and English, her father a Scot. Neil's father was half French and Irish. Later in his life Neil used to call himself the "League of Nations".

Neil's father was employed by the N.Z. Railways, usually in the capacity of Station Master. The family moved around New Zealand a great deal so he knew no permanent home until they went to live at Maungaturoto when he was about eight. After living in the heart of Wellington he loved the country life, and was fascinated by the birds singing early in the morning. He played a great deal on his own around the railway yards and was very interested in the stock yards, where he learned something of sexual mating. At school he was never very successful in subjects which held no interest for him, but came top in history and general knowledge. Like most children in those days, when radio was still in its infancy, he read a great deal in his leisure hours. He enjoyed sport and played all games well.

His father, William, was a very popular man who lived a selfish life, going to the club every night and saving no money. Emily, his wife, constantly complained about his shortcomings and the marriage was unhappy. In the early days of the great depression, a kind Government told William he had to retire early so they could cut down his superannuation; he was offered a job as manager of a hotel but Emily wouldn't consider such a position, so they moved to Auckland. Neil's brother Ken, who had been a boarder at Whangarei High School, was put on a farm to earn his keep at 50c a week.

In Auckland the family lived first in Morningside, and William tried unsuccessfully to get a job. He stopped going to the club, as he had no money to spend on his friends, and the family lived a very frugal life. After about two years he got a job as a tally clerk on the wharf, and was back in the club again every night.

Neil went to Grey Lynn School, passed his Proficiency exams, and attended Seddon Memorial Tech. for two years as a day boy. After this he started work in a garage for $1.50 a week, and had two further jobs before settling down working in a big store. At the same time he went to night school, and had one year part-time at Auckland University. He read widely and was particularly interested in psychology, sex and religion.

Until about 18 years of age he had been an altar boy and bible class teacher in the Church of England; then he read *The Martyrdom of Man* by Winwood Reade, and began to have doubts. After further reading of a rationalist nature he came to the conclusion he was an agnostic, which upset his mother very much. She blamed his friends for taking him away from the church, and he could never get it through to her that it was his own decision.

At the outbreak of war in 1939 he enlisted and went away with the Second Echelon to England, voluntarily, not for reasons of "King and Country" but because he believed New Zealanders had more freedom than the Germans. He was a good soldier, doing his job and making the best of all situations, but inclined to question the actions of his superiors and consequently made no progress in his military career. Twice he was wounded, and suffered several near misses, one of which showed him something of his inner qualities.

While sitting talking with his comrades, in the desert, suddenly over the escarpment came a Messerchmitt, very low, diving on their gun position. Neil saw the bomb drop and turned and dived into the slit trench. He knew it was headed in his direction, and as the noise got louder said: "Well, here goes!" — no prayers. The bomb landed at his head and blew away from him, filling the trench with rocks and sand. Later on, when he read in Orage's *Psychological Exercises* about "daily dying" he knew it was not always true to say a dying man sees his life pass before his eyes, because in the instance he experienced he had had only one thought: acceptance. It was to stand him in good stead later in his life.

He never attained any rank in the army, mainly because of dumb insolence to his officers. He was a prig, judged everyone, and did not learn from his experiences to accept ordinary life as he had accepted the possibility of death.

He saw action in Greece and the Western desert and was sent home on furlough after the collapse of the German army in North Africa. When he reported to go back to the war he was found to be medically unfit because of his wounds, so was suspended from active duty and put on reserve.

He returned to the store for a short while but decided to get a different job, so took a course in electric welding through the Rehabilitation Department, then worked for the Auckland Harbour Board for two years.

He had drifted into marriage with the fiancee of a friend who had been killed; he had visited his wife-to-be solely out of friendship, she was lonely, he started taking her out, and subsequently they married. The marriage was a disaster, but it taught him a great deal. Before he was married he had been given a premonition of what was to happen — while sitting on a beach in the moonlight he had seen his wife as she was to become twenty years later. During the courtship she occasionally acted in a very irrational manner but in his egotism he thought he could change her, and that everything would alter after they were married. As both were completely selfish, the marriage never stood a chance. It was an example of emotional love, one moment fighting, the next physically loving. He wanted children, she did not. However, after three years they had a son, and two years later a daughter.

Neil was ambitious. While working for the Harbour Board he started building a house in his spare time, completed it in a year, and started another. In this way he became a builder, in a few years employing a big labour force. His home life was chaotic. To survive, he had become dominant; his mother called him a bulldozer — a good assessment of his character.

Neil and his wife became friendly with another married couple; the inevitable happened and he fell in love with Rose, who represented the antithesis of his own wife, D. He said nothing to anyone of his feelings for a long time. Later on they were to be accused of immoral conduct, but the relationship was quite platonic. Both were too full of fear to be natural and both considered their children before their own happiness.

About this time Neil's father died, and after another year of bickering Neil left his wife and children to live with his mother. He tried to get custody of the children but D. played the innocent party, and after costly litigation a judge gave her custody and Neil reasonable access.

By the time he was 35, Neil had formed the opinion that life was futile and man was driven by the sex urge to accomplish most of what he achieved in the way of progress. His bible was Havelock Ellis's *Psychology of Sex*. One day when talking to a carpenter, he mentioned this belief that sex was the driving force in man. The carpenter disagreed and gave him a book by Paul Brunton, *The Hidden Teaching Beyond Yoga*, which he left on a shelf in his bedroom for a month and then was prompted to read. He had read *The Light of Asia* when a boy of 17, and was addicted to the *Rubaiyat* of Omar Khyam, although he did not understand its esoteric worth. Paul Brunton gave him a shock, and he started to look at himself in a new way. He got a taste of his egotism and selfishness, saw a little of the strength of his body, and began doing some of the exercises.

One evening at a master builders' party he got into conversation with a Jew who mentioned the names of Ouspensky and Gurdjieff, and, when he found what Neil was searching for, gave him an address where he could contact people who were also interested in these ideas. He made the contact and joined the group, which was led by a man who claimed he had met both Gurdjieff and Ouspensky. Neil attended the group for about five years then was asked to leave, as he was questioning the leader and his apparent imbalance.

He decided to start a group and contacted Mr. C. S. Nott, in England, to guide them. Seven other people left the original group and started working on themselves under Nott's instructions.

During this time, about five years after he had left D., Rose contacted him, and the result was that she left her husband and came with her three children to live with Neil and his mother. Neil's wife would not give him a divorce and complained to the court that he was living in sin, requesting that his children should no longer visit him or his mother at their home. The judge agreed to this; Neil told him he would no longer make footballs of the children and was not going to pick them up to go round some corner with them; if he couldn't have them to his house he would wait and see what eventuated.

Rose was upset at this turn of events as she knew Neil was very attached to his children, so she decided they should have a child, and after a year he arrived. This made his wife react in a savage way; she declared she would never give him a divorce and his children would be bastards.

Neil had now learnt something of external considering and felt for Rose's parents and his mother. Although he considered himself married to Rose in the

sight of God, he realised the consequences in the sight
of man. His wife became very vicious, harassing him as
much as possible. She successfully swayed his children
against him and was insistent and insatiable in her
monetary demands. His business had a bad year, his
so-called friends deserted him and he was forced into
liquidation. When he cut down on the maintenance, his
wife took him to court on the grounds of destitution.

Fortune looked after him and he struck an enlightened magistrate who told his wife that Neil was
doing his best under the circumstances. This was true,
as his wife was getting more than Neil out of the wages
he was on, and at the same time working and receiving
more than Neil's income.

After two years of want, a period Rose and Neil
called their depression, he started a business again and
became quite successful. They had two more children,
and when the divorce law was liberalised he obtained
a divorce, married Rose, and the children were
legitimised.

He had tried to make contact with the children of his
first marriage, and his eldest son had worked on his
building jobs in the holidays. Neil had paid for him to
go to Pharmacy School till he graduated as a chemist.
He tried visiting his daughter at home, but his former
wife then began saying he was tired of Rose, so he
stopped. His daughter had asked him to give them
another house and after he did this she ignored him,
neither inviting him to her wedding nor telling him she
was having a baby when it came three years later.

The way

During this time Neil had been working on himself and had a more tolerant attitude to people and life in general. He made plenty of mistakes but realised that the only people who don't are those who do nothing.

In 1963, on Mr Nott's advice, he visited Sydney to contact Mr Nott's Australian pupils and became aware they were on about the same level as the New Zealand group although the Australians were doing Gurdjieff's movements.

Much of what he was told by Mr Nott did not fit in with things he was doing within himself. They disagreed on several points in the Gurdjieff system. Because he was sincere in the search for the Truth, Neil had to put everything through himself, and would not blindly follow anyone. He came to the conclusion that Mr Nott was identified with the personality of Gurdjieff, because of his close contact with him. Neil did not judge him for this, but was more concerned with the Teaching than the teacher. He loved Gurdjieff and knew he was his guru, but did not want to become involved with other people's ideas of Gurdjieff. At the same time he was indebted to Mr Nott for what he had taught Neil of the Gurdjieff system. He was led to cry out to Gurdjieff for a lead to separate the chaff from the wheat and at the end of 1966 had a glimpse of things to come.

One evening when Rose and the children had gone out Christmas shopping, he was alone, pondering about the missing link in the Gurdjieff system from his standpoint, when he was prompted from within to go to his study and get what he called the "Paris papers". These were some unpublished questions and answers from Gurdjieff's meetings in Paris in 1941. When he picked them up they fell open at the line "Repeat, repeat, repeat. You forget. You have no memory. You never repeat enough. Try a little autosuggestion, keep repeating, repeating." Neil had studied auto-suggestion years before in a business course, and decided to learn about hypnotism.

He read Le Cron's *Self Hypnotism* and began to contact his subconscious mind with a pendulum. He tried for months to hypnotise himself, without success, and became aware that he had a deep-seated fear. Through the pendulum he learnt how to overcome this, and eventually was able to hypnotise himself. Then he carried out Gurdjieff's advice, and repeated. All year he hammered away, slowly eliminating many of his negative emotions that had beaten him during his life. He found out about the guide to his conscience, the goaffadh birds and the pitfalls associated with the use of the pendulum. After the meetings with the group he would find out where they had gone wrong and rectify it the next time. At this time they were studying Gurdjieff's *All and Everything* and this was where Neil, who considered himself not the teacher but the leader of the group, began to disagree with Mr Nott.

During 1967 Neil was trying to find out if there were any Men No. 5 in the world at that time. Through his pendulum he found there were and that he could contact them. As the pendulum gives only "Yes" and "No", finding the names presented a problem. Eventually he asked if he could find out through the books in his library and was given the affirmative. Taking each book in turn, he narrowed it down to Hazrat Inayat Khan's *The Sufi Message*, Vol. I, and Bennett's *Witness*. He wrote to the Sufi Movement of H. I. Khan and eventually received a letter from Mushraff Khan. Bennett's *Witness* was harder, as the pendulum said it was not Bennett, so Neil went through the book page by page until he found a reference to Ramdas in the footnotes. He wrote to Ramdàs and received the information that Ramdas had died a year or so before.

Neil began corresponding with Pir O Murshid Mushraff Khan and discovered he was the Man No. 5 who could help him. His pendulum told him that he must have a physical contact with Murshid Mushraff, so he decided to visit him in 1968. Every day when Neil sent Mushraff Khan his love, he received an answer in his heart. This went on for several months, until one day nothing happened. After two weeks a letter from Shahzadi Khan told him her husband had passed away. This caused Neil some concern as he had made arrangements to proceed overseas to visit Mushraff Khan and Mr Nott, as well as other Gurdjieff people and members of the Sufi Movement of H. I. Khan.

Neil's guide to his conscience was adamant that the trip should proceed, so at the end of March he left New Zealand to follow the promptings of his guide.

He flew by way of Tahiti and arrived at Mexico City, where he visited the Pyramids and was able to understand something of the Law of Three in relation to the teachings of the Aztecs. He had been given the name of a member of a Gurdjieff group to contact in Mexico and the rebuffal he received was his first encounter with the ignorance and secrecy of the Gurdjieff people. Gurdjieff's own conditioning had led him to caution in giving out his teaching, and this had been senselessly carried on by his followers.

A strange thing happened to Neil as he was walking past one of the Aztec ruins: a truck driver loading soft drink bottles dropped some, they broke in the air and a piece hit Neil in the back and drew blood.

From Mexico City he went to San Antonio and met the national representative of the Sufi Movement. That night, in the hotel, Neil woke up after sleeping for an hour to find the room filled with a very strong scent. He wondered idly if they put it through the air conditioner. Next day when he was initiated into the

Sufi Movement he smelt it again. Later he was to find out that other Sufis in the Movement had experienced this and believed it to come from H. I. Khan.

In America, Neil took a Greyhound bus from New Orleans to Spring Green, in Wisconsin, stopping over in Memphis on the day Martin Luther King was assassinated. There was great tension in the air, which was to follow him all over America. Mr Nott had told Neil to visit Mrs Wright, a pupil of Gurdjieff's in the early days, who had married Frank Lloyd Wright, the great American architect. They had a school near Spring Green, but on arrival Neil found they were in Arizona where they had another, winter school. This was the second time Neil had been on a wild goose chase and he wondered if he was wasting his time. While waiting for the bus he went for a walk down a side street and passed an old man leaning on his front gate. Neil said "Good day", the old man replied, and they started talking. Intrigued by Neil's accent, the old man enquired where he came from, and learned of his mission to Spring Green. The old man laughed and said Neil must have been led to the right place, as he had been Mr Wright's odd job man for more than 20 years. He then gave Neil a resume of the work that had been going on at the school, and his opinion of everyone concerned. It was an insight that could never have been obtained from any other source.

After a few days of travel to Canada, Neil arrived in New York, where he met some Sufis and had worthwhile talks. He also contacted Gurdjieff's people, but as it was Easter weekend most were out of town or not available. He had a meeting with Lord Pentland, the leader of the New York group, and found him compatible. Neil formed the opinion that apart from the movements, these people were no further ahead with the work on themselves than the Auckland group.

From the U.S.A. he flew to Holland and booked into a hotel at the Hague. Over the next fortnight he had many talks with Mrs S. Khan. The Dutch Sufis were marvellous to him and he made some real friends.

While in Holland he was told by his guide that he must go to Afghanistan to contact a Man No. 5, which amazed him as he knew no one in Afghanistan. When he told Mrs Khan, she said she knew an Afghani, a friend of her husband, who was at an institute in the Hague. One of the lecturers was a Sufi who had asked Neil to come and see him at this institute. Neil arrived to find the lecturer had been called away so was sent to the students' lounge, where he was soon in conversation with a group of people. He talked for a while with some Iranis; when they left a man came over and sat with Neil, saying "I can help you." It was the Afghani friend of Mushraff Khan. He hadn't known anything about Neil, but later told him he felt compelled to speak to him. The Afghani was returning home soon, and told Neil he would introduce him to some Sufis if he came to Afghanistan.

From Holland Neil went to London, where he was met by an ex-member of the Auckland group. Later he contacted Mr and Mrs Nott and went with them to their cottage in the country. The next day Mr Nott went to Bray, a centre of the Gurdjieff movement in England. As it was wet and cold, Neil and Mrs Nott talked most of the day. They were at ease in each other's company, and she told him many stories of Gurdjieff and Ouspensky.

Later Mr Nott took him to Peterborough, where he had a small group, and Neil stayed for a couple of days with one of the members. Before leaving New Zealand, Neil had been told by Gurdjieff that he would get the Third Series of Gurdjieff's essays, and during the course of conversation mentioned that he hoped to get a copy but didn't know where it would come from. Colin and Nigel said they could give him one, as they'd made duplicates of a copy obtained from Fritz Peters. At this time these copies were very rare and few of the new members had ever seen one.

Neil spent a month in England and visited the Gurdjieff people at Bray and Addison, where he was well treated. He was also able to meet a number of the

Sufi Movement followers, who received him well.

He arrived in France just as a major transport strike was starting, and during the next two weeks did a lot of walking. He met Madame de Salzmann and Henri Tracol, and had interesting talks with them. While in the Cathedral of Notre Dame, which he visited every day, he had strong inner insights which showed him the way he must take.

From France he went to Switzerland, then Italy, and met a number of the Sufi Movement members. Leaving Rome he went to Istanbul, where he visited a Dervish lady who introduced him to others, including two young men who guided him round the city. In Konya, where he went to visit the tomb of Rumi, he was looked after by several Dervishes. He saw them dance and felt at home with these wonderful people. One night one asked him why he was going to Afghanistan to find his teacher when he could get one in Turkey. Neil told him he was driven from within to take this course. The Dervish said that he must pray to Allah and ask Him to show Neil his teacher. Later that evening he did this and was shown a man with a sheet and a white beard walking past the window.

Neil travelled through Iran to Kabul, in Afghanistan, where he contacted his friend Hayatallah from Holland who made arrangements for him to meet Shaikh Ibrahim, a top Sufi Shaikh. At his house they were shown into a room and asked to wait with some other men. After a time a man entered, Neil was introduced, and all sat. A few moments later another came in and the procedure was repeated. Neil was told from within that this was where he was to meet his teacher, and as each man came in he looked at him expectantly, but none of these men were like the vision. Neil spent two hours talking to them. The Shaikh was a fine man and he and Neil got on very well together, but inside, Neil's state was utter turmoil, as he felt he had now proved it was only imagination that was driving him. Perhaps Mr Nott was right after all. In the depths of his perplexity he looked out of the window opposite and suddenly the man of his vision appeared, exactly as he had seen in Turkey two weeks before.

Shaikh Abdul entered the room and was introduced to Neil. He sat away from Neil and Shaikh Ibrahim, and said very little. After about an hour, Neil and his friend left. Neil told Hayatallah that the last man was the one he had come to see, but Hayatallah said they would have to wait a few days before approaching Shaikh Ibrahim again. After a week they visited the good Shaikh who explained that Shaikh Abdul had called only that one night, and that he lived in Kandahar. He gave Neil his address and wrote a letter of introduction. On the way back to Kabul, Shaikh Ibrahim's son said Shaikh Abdul had told them Neil was an unusual man. Hayatallah felt that the meeting with the Shaikhs was the most unforgettable night of his life. It was also very important to Neil.

On the way to Kandahar by bus, Neil stopped at Ghazni and visited Hakim Sana'i's tomb, which had a good atmosphere. Sana'i was a teacher of Rumi, highly venerated in Sufi circles. Ghazni, which Omar Khyam talks of when he refers to Sultan Muhamet on his throne, was once a great city, but now was a broken-down village.

At Kandahar Neil booked into a small hotel and contacted Amunallah, who was to be his interpreter. Amunallah promised to be there in an hour, but arrived three days later only after the manager of the hotel became irate and dressed him down, calling him a stupid man. However, later Neil found Amunallah to be a good man, a protector of the poor and an honest Muslim.

When eventually Amunallah was to take Neil to Shaikh Abdul's house, they found he had gone away to the villages and would not be back for some days. This caused Neil a bit of disappointment, and he struggled with resentments. Obviously Amunallah felt guilty about his delay in meeting Neil, so he volunteered to take him to the villages the next day to find Shaikh Abdul. He said he would be there at 6 o'clock.

That night, while saying his prayers, Neil sent a strong message to Shaikh Abdul.

Next morning Neil was waiting at 5.45 and had plenty of time to work on himself, as his interpreter didn't arrive till 7.45. Amunallah drove very fast, with his record player on at maximum decibels. He was fond of Arabic singing and had plenty of records to prove it. Neil liked the music as it reminded him of his Cairo days, but he found the noise trying.

After driving in this fashion for about two hours, Amunallah suddenly braked and said: "He has stopped me." Neil got out of the car and saw an old bus stop opposite. Next moment, out of the bus stepped Shaikh Abdul with his small case in his hand. Amunallah rushed over to him, took the case and kissed the Shaikh's hand. Neil followed suit. The Shaikh spoke to Amunallah in Farsi and Amunallah translated: "He says he got your message."

They climbed back into the car and drove off again, but this time there was no music or smoking; Amunallah told Neil he refrained out of respect for Shaikh Abdul. While they drove, Shaikh Abdul told Neil through Amunallah that he had wanted to take Neil away with him when he was at Kabul.

When they were seated back in Amunallah's house, Shaikh Abdul told Neil he would not speak to him until he had become a Muslim. This Neil agreed to undertake; they showed him how to perform wuzu and dressed him in clean white clothes, then Neil embraced Islam and performed his first Ra'akats, with Shaikh Abdul instructing him. Later Shaikh Abdul initiated him as a Naqshibandi Sufi. Neil was put in a room on his own and told to say a mantram while Shaikh Abdul investigated his heart.

Neil stayed with Amunallah, and Shaikh Abdul looked after his spiritual needs at his mosque, where several ceremonies took place. Neil was in a state of peace although his body was suffering from dysentery. He was praying all day and half the night, and Shaikh Abdul carried out many Sufi practices. They would sit together, each under his sheet, which kept off the flies, and communicate with each other via the heart. Later Neil checked the salient points by asking Amunallah to interpret, and found them quite accurate. Shaikh Abdul was very moved by what he had found in Neil and gave him the name Abdullah, which means "Slave of God." He told Neil that he had done more in three days than many people could do in twenty years, and that they were connected by someone close to Allah. He wanted Neil to stay with him permanently, and when Neil left for Herat at the end of two weeks, he promised to return some day.

From Herat he travelled to Mazar el Sharif and Balkh (called the "mother of all cities"), the birthplace of Rumi, then to Bamian, the home of two big stone Buddhas dating back to 200 B.C., where he found a marvellous atmosphere.

Returning to Kabul, he contacted Shaikh Ibrahim again, and stayed, as Shaikh Abdul had asked him, for two weeks. Shaikh Ibrahim gave Neil further instructions on the Naqshibandi way and the day before Neil was to leave, made him a Shaikh and gave him the name Isa.

After travelling through India, Pakistan, Hong Kong and Australia, Neil arrived home to be greeted by his family. He was much thinner and wiser than when he left, and felt happy to be home.

Preparation

Neil settled down to work again and was busy with life affairs. He told the Gurdjieff group, which numbered about 18, that he now considered himself to be the teacher. Because of this one member left after a few weeks, but most kept working for some time.

Neil introduced the ideas of Hazrat Inayat Khan and told the group there would be a Sufi meeting separate from the Gurdjieff meeting. A member offered his house, and the Brotherhood meetings started. After some time they decided to have Universal Worship, which was held at Neil's house every second Sunday. Eleven adults and 12 children were present at the first service.

Neil and Rose, who had been doing a fast once a week for some years, did their first Ramadhan and found it to be very helpful. Rose found Ramadhan easier than the Monday fast, but Neil suffered a great deal going without a drink so decided that from then on he would go without water on the Monday fast, to get some practice.

During 1969 the group membership stayed at about 20 and Neil and Abdullah concentrated the work on the body. All the group members fasted one day a week, and in July they tried a seven-day fast on water alone. One gave up after two days, another after six days, the rest completed it. During the fast they prayed together in the middle of the day and sent their thoughts to each other. The fast had a big effect on most of the members. One gave up working, as he said it was too tough for him. Another older member who was not interested in fasting didn't try, and subsequently gave up the group.

In this year Neil wrote a book[1] on these ideas with many others coming from Abdullah. The manuscript was sent to England and turned down by three publishers, so Neil was told from within to forget about it and wait until someone wanted to publish it without his soliciting. He sent a copy to Madame de Salzmann, who was noncommittal, only cabling to ask if she could keep it.

In the same year Neil had a visit from one of Mr Nott's Peterborough group. This man stayed a month and reported back to Mr Nott. Neil let him use his study, and after a few days became aware that he was systematically going through all Neil's private papers. From within, Neil was told to let this traitor carry on with his prying. Towards the end of his stay, Neil and Abdullah were told to put on a show for him. Neil and Abdullah had demonstrated what he called ESP for the group once before. The experience horrified the guest and he reacted as Neil had been told from within to expect. He sounded a big negative to Neil's positive and later wrote to the group denouncing Neil as a madman.

On the morning of Gurdjieff's birthday, in January 1970, Neil read this letter to the group and all were on Neil's side. This man also created a reaction from Gurdjieff people overseas. Madame de Salzmann ignored any correspondence, as did Pentland and H. Tracol. This put Neil out on a limb and forced him to do his own thinking. Obviously this was the best thing for Neil to develop on his own, as the Gurdjieff people were all too identified with Gurdjieff's personality, forgetting the parable of the workers in the vineyard. They gave lip service to Gurdjieff's injunction that one must think for oneself, while condemning anyone who

---

[1] *Probings,* correlating the ideas of Gurdjieff, Hazrat Inayat Khan and Abdullah, to be published shortly by Gnostic Press.

did just this. As Idries Shah says, this Teaching cannot remain the same for ever, although the knowledge is constant. The Teaching must vary with the teacher, although the way is the same. The intellectual and spiritual snobbery of the European adherents of the Gurdjieff system has put Gurdjieff's teaching into the Law of Seven and has created, in Gurdjieff's words, a number of Hasnamussians. Neil could not understand why Gurdjieff had left a woman in charge of his groups in France, but Abdullah knew. Neil was attracted to Madame de Salzmann and always defended her as being a courageous woman who was following what she considered to be the right way of passing on Gurdjieff's teachings; Abdullah saw much deeper than this.

Throughout 1970, membership of the Gurdjieff group, the Brotherhood of H. I. Khan and the Universal Worship, increased slowly. All year Neil did a lot of hypnotherapy for outsiders and members of his group. He never asked any payment for his services and tried to think he was working for God. Often his ego complained that people were using him, but most of the time he was able to overcome his inner considering. During this year he was prompted from within to paint his ideas, and kept constantly at this task in his spare time.

Early in 1971 Neil had an exhibition in an Auckland gallery and gave a talk on the ideas to over 100 people. He sold a few paintings and got a mixed reaction from the critics. Mostly the technique was taken to task; obviously few of the critics realised what he was up to. He was able to be objective and learnt a great deal about himself and his ego. He also began making screen prints of the ideas and had one accepted to tour New Zealand in an exhibition.

At the beginning of the year Neil's mother, who for some time had been interested in the ideas, had passed into a coma and remained thus for over eleven months. Neil was a constant visitor to the hospital and found it a great test in perseverance to sit by her side without any recognition from her. He found his love to be constant and missed seeing her only five days, two of which he was out of town. Lack of consistency had been one of Neil's great weaknesses and he now knew he had overcome this trait.

In 1972 the groups stabilised at about 30 members and the work on the body intensified. By 1973 the groups had grown to 40 and work proceeded at a good pace.

Neil was prompted to write about the ideas in music and completed the first three movements of the "Solar Suite" in the latter part of 1973. This meant he had given three mediums of expression to the Teaching as he understood it — a book, paintings and prints, and music. The fact that they had little success in the world did not upset him as he was living more and more within himself. At times his ego would get in the way but Neil now had become passive to Abdullah and it was mainly Abdullah who influenced the expression of the arts. Neil had become patient and knew from Abdullah that Allah's will will be done. During the last seven years Neil had been influenced by Ramdas a great deal and was happy at what Abdullah was doing. Abdullah had infused his own ideas into the Gurdjieff Teaching and the Hazrat Inayat Khan Message; thus the knowledge was taking another departure.

During 1974 the Gurdjieff group often had over 50 people at a meeting and there were over 30 at the Brotherhood meetings. The Universal Worship every alternate Sunday drew up to 100, half of whom were children.

This year Neil was told from within that he must return to Afghanistan for Ramadhan.

Prelude

In the two years preceding his departure for Afghanistan, Neil had been praying constantly: "Holy Father the Sun, grant that we may destroy the ego and become non-attached to the body and non-attached to our possessions." About three months before departure from New Zealand, "... and die to Neil" had been added. This addition caused Neil some consternation and now Abdullah had a block from Neil to contend with. Neil was happy at destroying the ego, but to sacrifice himself was a bit too much. Abdullah told him that this was the real meaning of the Christ on the cross. It is not the Christ as a man or teacher which counts, but Christ as a teaching. Neil had understood this for a number of years as a theory, but did not like it so much when he was going on the cross himself. This gave him a great deal more feeling for Rose, who was quite apprehensive about the journey. From now on Abdullah's prayers became harder as he was constantly harassed by the ego and directed by Neil. Fortunately Abdullah was strong enough to overcome this and although he did not win all the time, was always able to come out on top in the end. Saying the prayers was very difficult, and remembering on the hour more so. It was a strange situation because Neil knew that the ego must be destroyed and helped Abdullah with this task constantly, but resisted the idea of dying voluntarily. To give up Neil, who had taken such a long time to create, was a horse of a different colour.

The last three months before departure was a very

difficult time for all concerned, but Abdullah moved on relentlessly towards the fulfilment of his goal. He explained to Neil that although he had to die there would be left a residue, such as he carried of his past lives. Most of the time this conception satisfied Neil and he became more reconciled to his essential death on this scale. Over the last seven years he had been repairing two of his last lives by working on attitudes he had brought into this life as Neil.

On August 31 Neil left New Zealand with two of his pupils, Denis (Zaid) and Chris (Abdul), flying directly to Singapore where they stayed overnight before proceeding to Madras on September 1. They had to wait five hours at Madras before going on to Bangalore, and because there was no plane connection to Mangalore took a bus that left at night and travelled eight hours on a very bumpy roadway, then a train to Kanangad, the closest station to the late Swami Ramdas's Anandashram. This ashram was under the care of Mother Krishnabai and Swami Satchitananda, two of Ramdas's closest disciples. They arrived at the ashram by taxi on the morning of September 2 and were introduced to Mother Krishnabai and Swami Satchitananda. Each was given a clean room and had a small siesta, which Neil needed. He hadn't slept much since leaving New Zealand, on account of the time change. Neil's body seemed to need between four and five hours' sleep a night, and Neil believed, as Gurdjieff states, that one must give what is necessary for the planetary body.

The three were received in Mother Krishnabai's bedroom and each took a seat on the floor and faced her. She was sitting crosslegged on the bed, being given some medicine by Swami Satchitananda. A Dutch woman from Caracas, Venezuela was also sitting on the floor. Swami Satchitananda used a pendulum; the Dutch woman enquired and he put it on her. Neil observed that the pendulum was giving neutral and Swami Satchitananda came and sat with him and explained that he used the pendulum to diagnose. Neil told him he had also done this when he was practising hypnotherapy. Swami Satchitananda had a grave exterior but after a few minutes they were both laughing, talking about the death of the ego. Neil told Swami Satchitananda of his intended fast, and added that one had to be careful not to strengthen the ego by talking thus. Swami Satchitananda remarked with a laugh how deceitful the ego was and Neil agreed.

Mother Krishnabai was interested when Neil presented her with two of his prints which had been inspired by Swami Ramdas, "Victory to the Truth" and "Triumph to the Invincible Sun." She asked him to write out an interpretation of them and this is what Abdullah wrote:

"To understand these prints one must know the colour scheme adopted by Neil and Abdullah. White represents His Endlessness, the Whole Cosmos. Red represents the Lord of our Galaxy, the central Sun Antares or Ahura Mazda. A confusion comes with the use of Allah or Om, because the meaning depends upon the understanding of the speaker. Both can be used for His Endlessness, the Centre of the Galaxy, and also the Sun of our solar system. The Sun of our solar system is represented by orange. Green is the Earth. Blue is man. Purple is man's passions. Black is His Endlessness on the negative scale. Clear is His Endlessness in a reconciling fashion. Yellow is the atmosphere of the Sun.

"The top figure of 'Victory to the Truth' shows Om on the scale of the centre of our galaxy. The centre figure and the background to the top shows Om on the scale of the Sun of our solar system. The green figure at the bottom represents the Earth, and if you look closely you will see it is the same figure turned upside down. The background is the atmosphere of the Sun. The print endeavours to show that His Endlessness exists in everything as the Truth.

" 'Triumph to the Invincible Sun' shows how man can come up through his passions to a unity with God and that this can be done in our solar system only through our Sun; it is the atmosphere of the Sun that helps man to perfect himself. It also shows that the Sun is connected to His Endlessness through the Centre of the Galaxy. The seven purple figures show how man, to become freer, must follow the instructions of the Holy Lord Buddha and destroy his desires. If not, he will stay caught in the Law of Seven, the cyclic law, the law of life and death. The orange and yellow band coming down from the Sun shows that God will comfort and help man up to perfection if he balances the three parts of himself by his own efforts of going against his desires."

The main temple at the ashram had an inner shrine with a marble slab altar in the middle of which was a casket containing the relics of Ramdas covered with a cloth embroidered with "Om Sri Ram Jai Ram Jai Jai Ram." On the left-hand side the invocation was carved in a circle on a circular raised slab. On the right-hand side, also on a circular raised slab, was a representation of the soles of Ramdas's feet. A passage around the shrine had three portals at each side and one at each end, making another large room with an enclosed verandah cum passage. The men sat on the left side, women musicians in the middle played a harmonium, drums, finger cymbals and tambora, while other women sat on the right side. From 5 a.m. to 9 p.m. there was someone either singing or reading sacred books continuously.

Off the passage on the right was the wing which housed Mother Krishnabai. In the main temple was Papa Ramdas's chair and footstool, with a large photo set in glass, and on the right a smaller chair and footstool. High up around the walls hung photos of Hindu saints and one picture of Christ. In the sanctuary were photos of Ramdas's parents, Ramdas as a young man, and Ramdas as a Sadhu.

The life at the ashram had a pattern of devotion. The first service started at 6.30 a.m. and songs were sung for an hour. Flowers were brought in to Mother Krishnabai, who gave them to each person present.

The men first approached and prostrated before her to receive the flowers, which were in small chains, then slowly approached the sanctuary while all sang "Om Sri Ram Jai Ram Jai Jai Ram." They put their flowers around either the left or right marble emblem, then kissed the three parts of the altar. Some touched the photos and then their foreheads, as though blessing themselves with the darshan of the photo. They then approached the chairs and prostrated before them, some putting their heads on the footstools, others on the bottom of the chairs, each of which had on it a coloured paper lei arranged in the shape of a heart. After this they prostrated before Mother Krishnabai and, if he was present, Swami Satchitananda. Most then left, but the roster of singing kept on all day.

At 8 a.m. there was a one-hour service of continuous Ramnam, the singing of "Om Sri Ram Jai Ram Jai Jai Ram" to the same soft, lilting tune. This became very powerful after a time, and a feeling of peace stole over one. Many appeared to go into a state of self-hypnosis.

The next group prayers started at 11.30 a.m. and proceeded in a similar manner to the 6.30 service, except there were no flowers; a heart-shaped candle holder was lit while all sang praise to different saints. Then, starting with the men, each one held his hands over the flame and went through the same procedure in the sanctuary. After this they left the temple and were given prasad (blessed food) at the door, taking it in the right hand, not the left, as all good things should be taken in the right hand. This is also a Muslim custom as the left hand is supposed to be used to clean yourself after the toilet, and the right hand for eating food. Losing the right hand for stealing was a great tragedy because the thief could no longer feed with others from communal dishes.

The next session started at 3 p.m. and went on until 6.30 p.m., following the same pattern. Again this was repeated from 7 p.m. till 9 p.m. The women were given strings of flowers to put in their hair.

During the day people took darshan with Mother

Krishnabai and Swami Satchitananda in her room on the right of the temple. Although Mother Krishnabai was in a poor state of health she appeared to be still identified with the running of the ashram, and to know what she wanted. Servants constantly appeared at the door and window to be given instructions. When she was silent she gave off a feeling of peace, and constantly looked at a chair and footstool on which was a photo of Papa. People came in and prostrated before the chair and Mother Krishnabai. If they wanted to stay and take darshan they sat on the floor facing Mother Krishnabai, who sat crosslegged on a bed. If they had come for flowers, which she dispensed to the women, they prostrated and left.

After a few days Neil, Denis and Chris settled down to the routine and slowly became accustomed to the bowing and ritual of ashram life. Neil and Abdullah found the chanting of Ramnam very agreeable and often experienced moments of ecstasy. Abdullah had many talks with Swami Satchitananda and each recognised the other's sincerity. At first Mother Krishnabai was remote, but as the days passed she became very warm and close. She told Neil and Denis that Papa Ramdas was Allah's left hand; Abdullah explained to Denis later that really she should have said Papa was Allah's neutralising force, because he was one of the few people on the planet who had the third force of the Sun in them. On one occasion she asked Abdullah if he thought that Allah was in the ashram; he replied that He was everywhere, and the atmosphere in the ashram was conducive to anyone realising this. Mother Krishnabai was also very interested in the fast, and Abdullah explained that he saw a parallel between Papa Ramdas and himself, as both had been continuously driven from within. She nodded and smiled her smile. At this particular darshan Abdullah was very much aware of the presence of Sri Ramdas and commented on this to Swami Satchitananda, who relayed it to Mother Krishnabai. She agreed and looked hard into Neil's eyes, then smiled.

Abdullah and Neil were aware that both Mother Krishnabai and Swami Satchitananda had become Man No. 4. Abdullah could understand that although Mother Krishnabai and Swami Satchitananda were identified with the running of the ashram, their spiritual parts were able to make a break and separate life from spirit. Abdullah was able to meet with both Mother Krishnabai and Swami Satchitananda as an equal on the spiritual plane, although Neil was out of place because he was a man of action and quick movements, while Mother Krishnabai and Swami Satchitananda were more integrated with the slow-moving life parts of themselves. Neil had always bucked against bowing and scraping, as he called it, but Abdullah pushed him on to do this, as he knew behind the photos, chairs and altar was a conception of God which was pure and holy. Through Abdullah, Neil had become able to be contented in any place, as a discipline, and although Neil would rather have been at home with his family, he understood the purpose of the pilgrimage and acquiesced.

First octave

Day 1

Neil and Abdullah commenced the fast on the last day at the ashram, seven years after the birth of Abdullah. Physically it was as easy as the Monday fast Neil had observed for the last 21 years. Abdullah had been preparing Neil for a 40-day fast for six years, and the previous Ramadhan Neil had fasted on water alone for the last ten days.

Neil and Abdullah did Abdullah's prayers at 5 a.m., then at 6.30 Abdul, Zaid and Abdullah took Bhajan prayers at the ashram temple with Mother Krishnabai, Swami Satchitananda and many other devotees. Swami Satchitananda was insistent that Neil have a drink of coconut water before they left on the train from Kanangad, so Neil did, and afterwards told his companions he would be breaking the fast at the end of Ramadhan in the evening, so could have eaten all day if he had wanted to.

They arrived at Mangalore around noon and left for Bombay in the late afternoon after Zaid and Neil had tried unsuccessfully to mail parcels to New Zealand. Mailing a parcel in India is a major undertaking. First the parcel must be covered with a cloth sewn all round, then you have to fill in a declaration, the number of copies of which changes at each Post Office you visit. After this the parcel is weighed and you are sent to another counter for stamps. Usually there is a long queue at each counter with people pushing in quite regularly. The next step is to glue on one copy of the declaration and tie on one, two or three more. There is usually no glue available nor any string, so it is only experience that teaches what to be prepared for. The poor clerk doing the posting has several forms to fill in himself, and one gets the impression that this is bureaucracy gone mad. At Mangalore the clerk would not accept the parcels, as they were worth over 50 Rupees, and insisted on a clearance from the bank, which wasn't open. In Bombay, however, the parcels were accepted as they were, without bank clearance.

The three arrived at Bombay at 7.30. As they were proceeding to Jaipur next morning at 8, they decided to get a retiring room at the air terminal, but were told at the enquiry counter there were none, and they would have to go into the city to a hotel.

Swami Satchitananda had told them retiring rooms were available at Bombay, so they scouted around and eventually found them on the top floor of the airport. Neil suggested that the chap at the information counter must be getting a back-hander from the hotels. The retiring room was spacious but, like everything in India, run down. The three brothers agreed that the buildings in India appeared never to have had a coat of paint since the British left. There was no hot water, but they enjoyed a cold shower. The price for a two-bedded room was 72.60 Rupees, so Abdul elected to sleep on the roof of the building on a mat. Before retiring they found out their plane would not be leaving till about noon.

Abdullah told his friends that every day of the fast they might each ask him a question.

Zaid: "When living in close proximity to Neil and Abdullah Isa, a problem sometimes arises. Abdullah should be accorded respect in the form of obedience and acceptance at all times, because he is a spiritual teacher, but apart from normal respect and external consideration, it seems difficult and unnecessary to allow this same submission to Neil. If Neil appears to be irritable or mistaken about something, shouldn't the pupil speak out for himself, as long as he maintains conventional respect for an older man?"

Abdullah: "This question comes from vanity. It is unquestionable that Neil makes mistakes at times for a second or two, but they are always very quickly rectified by Abdullah. For Neil to gain a body kesdjan he had to work on himself for 21 years. He is a balanced man, and thus head and shoulders above an unbalanced one. Obviously in the course of the work on himself Neil has made a strong good part as well as an equally strong bad part. What happens is that the good part is strong enough to contain the bad, and there is a balance. The bad can be called the ego, the good the seed of Neil's individualisation — in other words, the beginning of his I. The idea of this fast is to destroy the ego and die to Neil, and create a much more powerful Abdullah."

Abdul: "Thinking of Mataji's illness — what is your general attitude toward the subject of karma? I noted that Swami Satchitananda gave some strength to this idea of the play, or lila, of God as being a separate way of dealing with the idea of 'Why the suffering?'."

Abdullah: "If we have had another life, we bring our karma with us. Some people are new souls, others old. If you are a new soul you have in you a goaffadh bird who has earned a chance as a human being. If you are an old soul then most likely you have had many lives, occurring about five hundred years apart, not, as the Hindus think, immediately after death. You also incur fresh karma in this life, therefore all your actions in this life count. Swami Satchitananda is right when he says all is the play of the Lord. He puts us in the right conditions to work on ourselves through our own actions. All is vibration; we develop within us a fine or coarse vibration depending on our work on ourselves. When we die physically, we are attracted to one of the planets of our solar system which is on a similar vibration. We stay there for about 500 years and are drawn back to parents on a similar vibration on this planet.

The 'we' Abdullah is talking about is our magnetic centre and deep essence from our previous lives. Illness is also attracted to us by our inner vibration, and Mother Krishnabai would have created the conditions long ago that result in her present poor state of health. Neil suffers for his resentment and negativeness of the past by having plenty of pain at times also."

Day 2

The second day of the fast started early with Abdullah and Neil doing their prayers at 5 a.m. The room was very hot but Neil felt well in the body, with no hunger pains or yearning for food. He did some washing and a little writing, then he and Zaid went to the Post Office, where they spent an hour learning a little more about patience and Indian bureaucracy, and sent their parcels to New Zealand. At 12.40 they caught the plane, arrived about 2 p.m. at Jaipur, and took a taxi to Ajmer where they stayed at a tourist bungalow. The room was large and a third bed was arranged. The shower didn't work but they were able to bathe under a tap.

In the evening Zaid and Abdul went out for a walk around the town to find Chisti's tomb, which was the object of the visit to Ajmer. Abdullah stayed at the bungalow, did some washing and went to bed at 8.30 but didn't sleep much as it was very hot. The temperature through the day was over 40°C. and over 30 in the evening inside a building. A great number of people slept out, which was much cooler, but Europeans preferred to sleep with their possessions, behind locked doors.

The heat was trying for Neil and the question of boiled water presented a difficulty. It arrived boiling hot, in the tea pot, and in the heat of the room cooled very slowly. As there was no plug in the wash basin it was difficult to cool the water with that method, so Neil found himself with lukewarm water which was not too palatable. Eventually he found a plastic bottle which he placed inside a small dipper used in Indian bathrooms to wash after defecation. The absence of toilet paper was something of a problem and Denis and Neil had been acquiring some in the planes, as it had been unprocurable in all the small places they had visited. From now on Neil would need very little.

Abdul: "Accompanying you on the fast, is there any other way we can help, for instance by fasting with you on day 7, 14 or 15, 21, 28 — I think we should fast from day 30 on to help?"

Abdullah: "The 40-day fast is for more than one purpose. Abdullah has told you of the aim to destroy the ego, die to Neil, become non-attached to the body, become non-attached to possessions, to gain Universal Vision by seeing God in everything existing and to fulfil the aim of the name Abdullah and become the Slave of God, serving Him without any thought of reward save doing His will. Abdul has divided things into seven through his conditioning from reading Gurdjieff on the Law of Seven. The Law of Seven is a cyclic law where eight becomes one again. On this level the 40-day fast is divided into five sections of eight, which gives five complete octaves. Each octave is for one sense: smell, taste, hearing, touch, seeing — not necessarily in that order. It is to create a special liaison between the body and the spirit which cannot be accomplished any other way. In regard to your help by fasting at different days, the best days are the third and the seventh of each eight days. If you want to do a long fast at the end, do the last eight days."

Zaid: "What are the effects of a period of time spent away from the teacher when a person is trying to work on himself?"

Abdullah: "It depends on type. Some people forget and go completely to sleep. Others, and they are few, use the lack of a teacher to act as a shock and work very hard on themselves. Hazrat Inayat Khan tells that when he was in America first a man and his wife visited him in a small town he passed through, and he gave them one exercise. He passed again many years later, and these good people had kept at the exercise faithfully. He was able to complete in one week what they had commenced, and they became enlightened. If a person is away from his teacher he can find another, always remembering that his first is contained in all subsequent ones. All gurus are God to the real pupil. You can see this in a country like India, where humility and devotion are engendered in the young, but in New Zealand this doesn't apply, as we are all taught that Jack is as good as his master. Many New Zealanders have so much fear that they kowtow to money and the wealthy with the hope of reward. We all know how much crawling goes on in the executive field, with the wives acting as a spur. So you see there are three answers to your question."

Day 3

Neil had a reasonable night's sleep under the circumstances. He was awake a lot and drank a pot of water through the night. Abdullah prayed a great deal and Neil and he did Abdullah's prayers at 5.15. Neil felt well in the morning and not hungry.

They left early and arrived at Chisti's tomb at 9.15. Abdul and Zaid had contacted a descendant of Chisti who was going to guide them. Chisti, who was known in India as Hazrat Khawaja Ghareeb Nawaz, was born in Isfahan, Iran, in the year 1136 A.D. The name of the shrine was Dargah Sharif, and the companions had trouble finding "Chisti's tomb", as they called it. The tomb was in the middle of four mosques, one of which, Akbari-Masjid, was built by the great Akbar. Another, Mehfil-Khana, was presented by Nawab Bashiruddula of Hyderabad. The third, built by Shah Jahan, was known as Juma-Masjid. The fourth was very small.

The guide took them to the tomb which they all agreed had a very good vibration. The top of the casket was covered with rose petals and pilgrims were constantly coming in with more. They also brought ornate cloths to be presented to the tomb and the guide explained that these were presented later to mosques all over India. Neil and Abdullah felt moments of ecstasy while praying at the silver rail around the body. Everything was either silver or gold; the guide showed them many things given by Akbar and the Nizam of Hyderabad. A very ancient copy of the Koran was treated with such reverence as it was being opened and handled that all were affected. The guide explained that this copy of the Koran had been made by Chisti's own hand, and pointed out Chisti's personal seal on one of the front pages.

That evening the companions attended Isha prayers in a marble mosque that had been built at the order of the Nizam of Hyderabad.

There is no doubt that Muslim prayers are masculine, and there is a sense of brotherhood not usually found in Christian assemblies. It is also true that a certain amount is done for show and that the majority of Muslims are motivated by fear, only a small number by faith and conviction — by conviction is meant love of God and man, irrespective of caste, colour or creed. The Muslim religion is very beneficial for emotional men if they are trying to balance themselves. It can also be helpful for a woman, as she has to practise it on her own without the attention of men; thus if she does her prayers she will attain sincerity.

Abdul: "In a place such as Chisti's tomb, what are the influences that can help a devotee; are they mostly in his own inner attitudes or to what degree does Chisti or his vibration help?"

Abdullah: "It is obvious that the state of the supplicant will influence the response. The majority of people who go to these tombs are after something for themselves. If they are emotional they can dream up with their imagination all kinds of effects in themselves. The correct attitude in going to such a shrine is to be passive and allow the vibrations to soak in without making conditions. Chisti was a Man No. 5. His bones won't help you; however, he has elected to help people who go to the shrine when he is there in the spirit. He was not there when we attended. The ecstasy Abdullah experienced came from our Holy Father the Sun. It is an unfortunate fact that millions of people put great store in relics such as bones of saints. In esoteric teachings it is universally recognised that the body belongs to the earth and is only the house of the spirit. When at any shrine it is correct to pray for others and permissible to pray that one may learn to serve God without seeking any rewards."

Zaid: "The first step when trying to practise brahmacharya would seem to be refraining from intercourse and lustful thoughts. What is the next step?"

Abdullah: "To practise brahmacharya one must work on lust, anger and greed. If one stops intercourse then this is the beginning — however, if one still struggles with thoughts of intercourse this undoes the physical abstinence. Many people who have no intercourse never reach perfection, while there are a number of people who understand and have intercourse, who do. This can be done by having intercourse with no lust or greed. To have balanced love in marriage each partner must consider the other's wants and this may necessitate sexual love. If this is done correctly then brahmacharya is not broken. The best way to overcome lust, anger and greed is to practise Ramnam, the repetition of some mantram invoking God by any name you wish."

Day 4

Neil had a fitful night's sleep but woke in the morning with no stomach pains or pangs of hunger. He and Abdullah did their prayers at 5 a.m., and in the long periods of lying awake did Ramnam constantly.

The companions left Ajmer at 9 a.m. and drove through part of the desert of Rajasthan to Merta City, where they were shown to the ashram of Muniji. They were expected as Bill, one of Abdullah and Neil's pupils in Auckland who had spent two months at the ashram, had written in advance.

The ashram was fairly primitive and Abdullah suspected it was kept so on purpose by Muniji to create conditions for working on oneself. As his name conveys in Hindi, Muniji had taken the vow of silence. He was a jolly man of medium build, with laughing eyes, who ruled with a rod of iron, conveying his commands by gestures. He had with him a Swami who was loud of voice, big of body, and talked incessantly. Muniji communicated with the New Zealanders by using a book, rapidly turning pages then putting his finger on a line and slowly moving it along. He mainly used the *Bhagavad-Gita*, and after a short while Abdullah and he were on each other's wave lengths. He offered them coffee and Abdul and Zaid were pleased to get a drink. Neil asked for boiled water. They tried to explain the fast but it took several hours before he understood. Muniji wanted Neil to take fruit juice with the water and thought Neil was fasting for four days. Later, when the idea of the fast got across, Muniji was very interested and he and the Swami were most helpful. The intense heat tired the brothers and shortly after sunset they arranged to sleep outside. Zaid and Neil were contented lying looking at the stars, and welcomed the cool breeze. It was very moving for Abdullah.

Zaid: "When in the company of one's teacher and a meeting occurs with another teacher of possible similar development, how should the pupil behave? Is it best to just listen to the conversation of the two balanced men and try to learn, without having much to say himself?"

Abdullah: "It is best to listen, because in this way you may become more detached. If you try to butt in then you will be clouded by your own ideas. By being silent you will learn more. As you know, it is by gaining inner silence that one has the possibility of hearing God within."

Abdul: "There is much poverty and misery to be seen in India, and a lack of interest in keeping things clean and operational, particularly public utilities, which itself contributes to the misery by helping to breed disease. Why is this so when India shows such signs of spiritual awareness?"

Abdullah: "This earth is a pain factory to sustain, by negative vibration, the moons and other planets. If there were enough conscious people on the earth this would not be necessary. Misery comes from the identification with the body as being the self. It is correct to give what is necessary for the physical body, but not to indulge it. Because some people have it easy, then others must have it difficult. The poor of India are in this category. India is an emotional country where there is very little intellect — people feel instead of think. If they thought, they would see the stupidity of many of their actions and take measures to correct the physical mistakes. However, you must not lose sight of the fact that many things that appear stupid to us are practical under these circumstances. One can come to God only by voluntary suffering, but in India, as in New Zealand or anywhere else, most suffering is involuntary. When poverty is practised in a voluntary way it is ennobling, but here, in an involuntary way, it is debasing, as can be seen in all the beggars snivelling for alms. The people of India have been looted by the British and now the Indian capitalist."

Day 5

Neil slept very little; he heard the clock strike every half hour through the night. However, he was refreshed by the cool breeze. Abdullah prayed all night and said formal prayers with Neil at 4 a.m. Neil had a queer taste in his mouth and a bit of wind, but felt free from hunger. He wrote most of the morning, and felt the heat a great deal. Zaid helped to work on a new garden and Abdul slept. At midday they went to an ancient tank and had a refreshing wash although the water was dirty. Back at the ashram Neil sat under one of the taps which surrounded the main water supply and rewashed himself. During the afternoon he sat behind the tank and cooled himself with a dripping tap, wetting his feet, head and hands, and in this way kept reasonably comfortable — you could not say cool, as the temperature was over 40 °C. and the breeze seemed to come out of an oven.

Once the sun was casting a shadow, Neil moved outside, laid out his bedroll on the tarpaulin supplied by Muniji, and slept for an hour from sheer exhaustion. Muniji and Swami were very kind to him, taking his pulse and placing their hands on his heart, which was in good order. Later Muniji gave Neil a drink of Ganges water, which they believed to have special qualities. Muniji told the brothers that Neil should stay until the eighth day of the fast and Abdullah agreed; in fact this is what he had recommended in New Zealand when they bought their air tickets.

Zaid: "Could you please speak on the subject of living in the moment, and about the awareness and observation necessary to practise this effectually."

Abdullah: "Many people confuse living in the moment with the disease of tomorrow or, in other words, 'let's live it up and to hell with what's going to happen later.' Mainly their idea is to satisfy their desires of the moment. To live in the moment is a big thing; you may get the taste from the mantram 'In the ever present here and in the eternal now', which is another way of saying God. If you want to learn to live in the moment you must have faith and trust in God. You must realise that everything on the planet is the lila of God, and if you have faith and trust then whatever conditions you are in are the best for you. The Holy Prophet's injunction must also be remembered — 'Trust in God, but hobble your camel'. You see we are doing that here, in this situation which is foreign to our usual conditioning. While Neil sits behind the shade of the tank and puts water from the dripping tap on his head, wrists and feet, thus maintaining a reasonable body temperature, Abdullah prays constantly. Neil is entitled to look after his body because the great heat and no food would tax his heart unnecessarily."

Abdul: "What are the forces at work in Muniji's ashram? Outwardly there is hardly anything of the comparatively elaborate ritual of Ramdas's ashram, and from observation of his pupils it's hard to guess what is flowing underneath."

Abdullah: "Muniji is teaching through austerity and the Gita. He makes the conditions tough, living out here in the desert. They teach a great deal of the time — you can hear the Swami droning on somewhere all day. He uses Ramnam, and by having so many boys on the ashram is also using the idea of Ramakrishna — he believes it is wise to get them young and keep them away from ordinary life, although of course they go to the ordinary school. They go to bed at about 9 p.m. and start the day at 4 in the morning. Muniji is all love and kindness to everyone, but stands no stupidity. He is a genuine man of God who is working well within his conditioning, and Abdullah respects and loves him. He makes his boys do the menial jobs, as Rumi did — you have seen them in the garden in the heat of the day. He teaches them how to do service with love for God and the recipient."

Day 6

Neil slept better in the cool breeze that blew through the night and joined Abdullah in his prayers at 5 a.m. His body was quite well and there was no hunger, although his mouth felt unpleasant. He wrote all morning, had a siesta for over an hour at midday, then spent two hours behind the tank. Muniji kept bringing Neil and Zaid books and showing quotations applicable to what Neil was doing. Neil, Abdullah, and Zaid to a lesser extent, were well aware of the ideas he expressed and had no criticism of them at all. Muniji spoke a lot about Bill and showed the brothers bits of letters. When Zaid and Abdul went to the village, they were asked about Bill many times; he seemed to be well regarded by all. He had helped the boys in the ashram with their science, biology and mathematics and all were very grateful. In the evening Abdullah talked to some English-speaking people about Sufism. Later the boys massaged and fanned him, as it was still very hot with no breeze at all. It became cooler after 10 and Neil slept very peacefully until 2.

Zaid: "The aim to date has been fairly general — 'working on oneself'. But now that certain steps have been taken, and certain acceptances made about future conduct, should the aim be more specific, even more pinpointed than learning to serve without seeking rewards?"

Abdullah: "Your specific task is to work on lust, wrath and greed, as it is for most people. This presupposes that one is also making the body obedient. If one works on these things one has some hope of gaining balance in the three brains. Learning to serve without seeking any rewards is spiritual work on the highest scale. This should be your spiritual aim, along with doing Ramnam. When one speaks about 'work on one's self', which is a very popular expression, one has to decide what is meant by the word 'self'. In Hindu philosophy the self is the Atman, but in Western popular ideas the self is the body, or ego. To Abdullah the self is your deep essence and whatever development of soul you have created."

Abdul: "It seems there is a growing spiritual awareness in the West. Would this be coming from the type of souls being reborn on the planet or from other factors?"

Abdullah: "The spiritual awareness in the West started at the end of the nineteenth century with Vivekananda. He was the man who gave the West its first conscious shock for many years. He was so catholic in his teachings that he left the way open for Zen, Sufism, Taoism, etc. to percolate through the Western society. In the *Bhagavad-Gita* Krishna says that when the 'dharma decayeth I come to help'. This is what has happened. God has sent a number of men to show the way and although there is more materialism, to wit such countries as Russia and

China, there is also as strong a religious revival, therefore the materialism is being contained.''

Day 7

Abdullah prayed from 2 a.m. and Neil joined him at 4. He had spent a good night and was very well and not hungry. He had the usual fur in his mouth.

Abdullah read the Gita for some time then wrote for two hours until Neil was asked by Muniji to come into his cell. Neil began to show Muniji a passage in the Gita, but Muniji bade him lie down; another man sat on the floor by Neil and prepared to take his blood pressure and test his heart. It touched Neil a great deal to think Muniji was so considerate as to arrange this on the seventh day. The doctor found Neil's blood pressure and heart to be normal, much to the relief of Zaid and Abdul. When they enquired how much to pay the doctor, Muniji said he was a disciple of his and there was no charge.

Muniji told the brothers he wanted to see them off and would make arrangements to get them to Merta Junction by bus. He also said he would arrange train reservations, as there was no connection with their flight to Delhi.

In the evening he tested Abdullah by imploring him to take some fruit juice. He used many arguments via a young boy called Bihari who translated from Muniji's gestures, and also used passages from the Gita. Abdullah pointed out a passage showing how Krishna loved anyone who had conviction. Muniji smiled and said via Bihari that Abdullah was a Mahatma, then went on to tell them that he had fasted on Ganges water for months. He also used to sit in the sun, with fires burning around him, until sometimes he blistered.

Muniji had one of his people explain about Merta City, an ancient town established 400 years before Jodpur was founded by Raojodha, which remained the capital of Marwar for many years. It gave birth to many warriors and saints of all creeds, and renowned battles were fought there. In the past it was a centre of cultural activities of Jain, Muslim and Hindu saints. The most famous was Mirabai, the female devotee of Lord Krishna. The city became deserted during mediaeval times and now seemed to be rising again, mainly through the existence of Shri Dutta Mandir Sanyas Ashram under the auspicious guidance of Sanyasi Saint Guru, 1008 Brahamnist Sadguru Shri Muniji-maharaj, with the assistance of his disciple Sri Durganandagiri.

The ashram is not only the seat of Vedic knowledge but is also a repository of other religious teachings. Many people of all castes and creeds, including a cadre of the top saints, come to learn "something" and thus satisfy their religious thirst. Many disciples of Guru Muniji are spread throughout the world.

Abdul: "Do you see the Indian-Middle Eastern area as being a reservoir of essential spiritual teaching, and would this account for the fact that most Western spiritual teachings appear to be essentially Eastern borrowings?"

Abdullah: "The inner teachings of all present religions come from the original Zoroaster. We believe there have been three teachers who have been called Zoroaster, or Zarathustra, to give them their Persian name. The earliest was about 5,000 B.C. The teachers of Vedanta visited him, so many people believe the Hindu teachings to be the earliest. We can trace Sufi teachings back to Abraham and the Essenes on one hand, and the Gnostics on the other. However, the Egyptians and Babylonians also had inner schools teaching these ideas. There is no doubt that the central spiritual knowledge came from the Middle East and has been fostered in many of these countries, so that Western men of discernment are led to the source."

Zaid: "The Indians, both local citizens and past pupils, who visit Muniji's ashram, show reverence and respect by removing their shoes when approaching him, kneeling or prostrating before him and touching his feet and then their hearts. This of course is not in our tradition.

The *Bhagavad-Gita* lays great stress on the correct way to approach the guru and shows many different aspects of this act of humility. What should be contained in our own approach to our own guru in our own country?"

Abdullah: "Ours must be from ourselves. If it is not genuine then better forget all about it. As New Zealanders we find this kind of show strange, yet we see people kowtowing before bishops, the Governor-General and the Queen. As New Zealand is a very Godless country there is very little stock put on spiritual attainments. People think that if they believe Jesus died for them then they are 'saved'. In New Zealand people mainly worship material attainment, and the wealthy, the famous footballers, etc., get what in India would be given to the guru. We must set our own standard, and it doesn't have to include bowing and scraping. The bows should be from within and the respect genuine appreciation of what the guru has gone through. This is all that is necessary."

Day 8

Neil had a good night's sleep, waking at 2 a.m. and saying Abdullah's prayers at 3.30. Neil was happy under the stars in the cool morning, and was reminded of his days as a soldier in the Middle East. He had his first dream about food. He had dreamed very little for some time now.

In the dream he was a boy in the back of a large truck backing at a furious rate. Lots of goods were falling off, among which were tins of food. He saw that another truck was rapidly going to crash into the one he was in, and decided to jump in a relaxed fashion into oblivion. Next, his mother was about to settle the damages claim when his father increased it to $10,000.

Muniji had been trying to make sure that Abdullah would come back in two months, but Abdullah would not guarantee this as he didn't know what would happen after Ramadhan and the Hajj. All morning, people came to talk to the three brothers. At midday they had a bathe under the tap that was being used to water the garden, and Neil sat behind the tank in the early afternoon heat, dousing his head and feet until it was time to go.

They left Muniji and the ashram at 3 p.m., accompanied by many people, and walked to the railway station. Neil and Abdullah did not turn around to wave; they had embraced Muniji shortly before they left, when Muniji wanted a photo taken of them together. The walk in the heat was tiring but Neil was feeling well. Several friends accompanied them on the train to Merta Junction. Things were going too smoothly, so complications now arose, the first being that the tickets bought by Muniji's man were for the following day. A Railways official said they'd have to wait until the next day, but Neil told the boys to jump on anywhere and see what happened. Neil entered an airconditioned coach, telling the attendant he would pay extra. The train had now started, and when the guard entered he told Neil he would have to pay about 200 R. Neil had only 100 R and the guard refused to accept his American traveller's cheques, but said he could have a 1st Class seat for under the 100 R. Abdullah thought Allah had decided Neil would be too comfortable in the airconditioned coach so was testing him again by putting him under stress. The 1st Class compartment, shared with two Indian Army officers, was fiercely hot until near midnight. Neil wet his head with a handkerchief to bring the body heat down. Zaid and Abdul found 2nd Class accommodation and brought all the luggage to Neil's compartment, where they sat for some time. They were passing through arid dusty desert so the windows had to be kept closed for several hours, which made conditions in the carriage hideous. Abdullah told Neil that everything is done for some purpose, and Neil and the body accepted this.

Abdul: "Observation of the life of the women in the Muslim quarters of the towns we have passed through so far seems to indicate that they lead a very hard life — bearing children, doing heavy manual labour and having to undergo the severe limitations of purdah. You have indicated that the Muslim faith has a lot to show women regarding their correct role. Could you explain further?"

Abdullah: "You are identifying with the outer manifestations of life in India. The Hindu women also fulfil the functions you say, of being slaves to their families. This is the shame of India and it is for the Indians themselves to correct. They have thousands of years of this conditioning to overcome in a hurry unless they want Communism.

"The Holy Prophet lived when people treated women and girls much worse than you see today. He lifted up the role of women by many injunctions in the Koran. All Muslims are not good Muslims, any more than all Christians or Hindus are exemplary. If you visited Greece, Italy, Ireland, among others, you would find that except for purdah, the women of the poor classes fulfil exactly the same role as these Muslim women. Although it is cruel, it does make women passive; what is lacking is intellect on the part of the men. All these people are motivated by fear. These men are active mainly through selfishness and fear, whereas if we are to be balanced it must be done through love and intellect."

Zaid: "I have difficulty in praying out of love and because of a wish to pray. Prayer often comes through the day out of a sincere wish to pray, but evening and morning prayers are often performed as a duty and a discipline. Will consistency help to make a change in attitude?"

Abdullah: "Yes. If you want to learn to play the piano you must practise. When people find it hard to do one of these disciplines then they must find out where the blockage is coming from in themselves. It may be from ego, body, vanity and conceit, laziness, inattention, or identification with some other thing such as bed, sex or tiredness. When you pray spontaneously through the day, this is coming from the spirit and the emotional part of yourself, and should be fostered as much as possible. If this is done, then the same part will be able to do the prayers at a set time morning and night.''

These first eight days were for taste.

Second octave

Day 9

After midnight the dust of Rajasthan was left behind and the rest of the trip was pleasant. Abdullah and Neil said their prayers very early, as the officer had told them they would arrive about 6 a.m., but a derailment held them up for two hours and it was about 9 when they got off at Delhi. They booked into a hotel near where Neil thought the tomb of Hazrat Inayat Khan was located.

Neil had the luxury of a hot shower, did some washing, shopped, and had a swim in the hotel pool. He felt well but tired, and slept soundly that night from 9 till 12.

Zaid: "What is behind the particular quality of a guru's method which seems to require the question and answer system as a means of imparting teaching?"

Abdullah: "It allows the teacher to keep a close check on the progress of the pupil and is used in conjunction with other methods, such as Abdullah putting you and Abdul together. For any progress there must be struggle; where there is no struggle people go to sleep. Questions give a good indication of a pupil's state, especially his identifications, limitations and attachments. When Abdullah sees you are getting too screwed up on one tack he directs you on another, thus helping you to find some balance."

Abdul: "To what degree does the law of fate operate on

a man once he has started to work on himself? I'm thinking in terms of the events leading up to the pilgrimage and how inner purposefulness operated which was not discernable at the time, or certainly not till the later stages."

Abdullah: "All life on earth is the lila of God. The law of fate operates in the moments you are conscious, so you can see it ebbs and flows with the law of accident in the majority of people. The more you are conscious, the more you are under the law of fate. There is, however, another force much stronger than either of these laws, that can affect anyone — no-one knows why. The force is grace. You were led to this Teaching by the grace of God, and this should engender in you a real feeling of humility and gratitude towards Allah. The way to repay is to work hard on yourself and learn to serve without seeking any reward but doing His will."

Day 10

Neil slept very little after midnight so Abdullah was able to pray most of the night; Neil joined him at 5. Neil drank a lot of ice water through the night. He and the body were happy to indulge in the cool water after drinking hot or lukewarm for so long. The body was well and not hungry, but Neil was not going to tax it too much in the hot sunshine of Delhi so told Zaid and Abdul they would start early to seek out Hazrat Inayat Khan's tomb. At the information office no one was very clear about where it was, but one man gave a general direction. Neil had been there seven years before, but in a taxi, and had no idea of the actual location. All he remembered was that it was very close to a tomb of a Sufi saint.

After walking a way they hired a three-wheeler which took Zaid and Neil to a tomb Neil realised was the wrong one, so they headed back the way they had come. The man at the hotel had said it was down a narrow lane, which Neil also remembered. After walking another half hour Zaid enquired at a post office; an old man told him he knew of the tomb and after a few minutes supplied the address. Another three-wheeler brought them to a very broken-down neighbourhood which Neil recognised as more appropriate. One of a group of young men knew of Hazrat Inayat Khan's tomb and asked the brothers if they would like him to show them there, adding that he attended meetings at Miss Hayat Bouman's house. Neil had been trying to contact Hayat since he arrived but always got an engaged sign at the phone number he had been given. The young man offered to lead them to her house, which was nearby. Neil had met Hayat when last in Delhi and had brought her two prints which she was pleased to receive. It appeared her phone had been withdrawn, as it was only a six-month rental. Abdul had already met Hayat when he was out walking. As she was European he had enquired about Hazrat Inayat Khan, and she had brought him home.

She gave Neil a drink of cool water and the brothers coffee, then took them to the tomb, where she left them. The tomb was modest, situated in the midst of poverty with open sewers and broken-down houses around, but was sheltered by a large tree and had a very good vibration. The brothers lit some incense and put rose petals on the cask, which was covered with an orange drape.

Neil had a letter of introduction from a Muslim brother in New Zealand to a Maulana whose mosque was situated close by, so they walked back and entered this mosque. The Maulana, who was very orthodox, was endeavouring to get a revival of Islam throughout the world. The brothers were well received, and the Maulana asked them to stay at the mosque. By now it was 12.30 and very hot; Neil was getting tired but he made no protest. Abdullah and the Maulana seemed to understand each other, although Abdullah sensed that the Maulana was condescending to the brothers, so he looked hard into his eyes, which the Maulana averted.

Shortly after, they left and made their way to Thos.

Cook's to pick up mail and confirm their flight to Kabul. Although they had reserved from New Zealand, they were told they were wait-listed.

Zaid and Abdul had lunch in Delhi and Neil returned to the hotel, where he had a swim and sat in the sun for about two hours, with the result that he was a little dizzy when he stood up. However, the faintness passed in a few seconds so he read and wrote until going to bed at 10. He slept only two hours.

Abdul: "Do you think Islam is going to be able to break out of the rigid formalism such as we observed in the Muslim centre we attended today?"

Abdullah: "The brand of Islam witnessed today is founded on fear, reward and punishment. It is archaic and must slowly lose ground to a more liberal form. These people are wrapped up in the letter rather than understanding the principle behind the words of the Holy Koran. Religion founded on fear, reward and punishment contains the seeds of its own destruction, thus it can only perpetrate more misery in the world. Islam means peace; it has a great deal to offer the world as well as individuals if they will listen to the inner teaching."

Zaid: "It seems that a disciple is one who is committed to a discipline."

Abdullah: "When you are a disciple you must obey the teacher's instructions, thus putting yourself under a strong discipline. You must have trust in the teacher and realise that if he is a true teacher he has no axe to grind for himself, rather he is considering your welfare all the time. He is putting himself under strict discipline constantly, so you must follow his example."

Day 11

Neil was up very early for prayer with Abdullah, who had been praying since midnight. As it was the first day of Ramadhan, Neil was making sure he had plenty of liquid and drank a pint of water before daylight. He felt very well and accompanied Zaid on a walk for an hour, then stayed in his room and wrote for an hour. Later he had a swim, resumed writing for three hours, and read a book until 9.30. He had his longest sleep so far on the trip, awaking at 2.30.

Zaid: "We talk about external considering of others and see that it is a correct way of working, but it seems to require a special effort to remember to put it into practice. Our ingrained habit patterns of selfishness operate almost automatically and block external considering a lot of the time. What is the best way of cutting through this?"

Abdullah: "Remembering God is the only way — by Ramnam, Zikr, prayer, or trying to see God in the person you are trying to consider. External considering of others is one of the hardest disciplines a person can undertake because it brings in the three brains simultaneously. When we find fault in others and resent them, we often find on reflection that what upsets us in the other is to be found in ourselves — often in a very grotesque fashion — and this must be used to heighten our own understanding of ourselves. Another way of learning to externally consider is to realise that the person concerned is only the outer manifestation of the varying degree of spirit within. Some may have no magnetic centre, others may have one, others a soul, and so on up the scale of perfection."

Abdul: "It's intriguing to see the Law of Seven in its repetitive sense cropping up in a spiritual organisation where bickering and arguments over leadership seem to occur, for example in the Gurdjieff and Hazrat Inayat Khan movements. Why does this happen and what factors prevent Gurdjieff or Inayat Khan from passing on the mantle of leadership with fewer complications?"

Abdullah: "Your answer is in the question. It is the Law of Seven. Both Gurdjieff and Hazrat Inayat Khan appointed people to carry on this work. Madame de Salzmann still runs the Paris Gurdjieff group, and some in England and the United States. Hazrat Inayat Khan appointed his son Vilayat as his successor, but died when the boy was young so his brothers took the leadership. The main split in the Hazrat Inayat Khan movement took place when Pir O Murshid Mushraff Khan died, as he appointed his nephew Fazal the next leader. As far as Abdullah is concerned it is not the teacher that matters so much as the Teaching. This does not mean to imply that Abdullah does not love and venerate both Gurdjieff and Hazrat Inayat Khan, but he realises that their Teaching is much bigger than either man, however developed he may be."

Day 12

Neil was up early and said the prayers with Abdullah. He felt very well, and did his packing and some writing. Hayat Bouman visited him and they discussed the situation between Fazal and Vilayat. Abdullah summed up by saying that until he had an opportunity of meeting both men he could express no opinions, but felt there must be some amicable solution to the problem. Both Abdullah and Neil were very touched by the thoughtfulness of Hayat in coming to visit him before his departure, bringing a rose from Hazrat Inayat Khan's tomb for good luck.

The three brothers arrived at Palam airport to find they were wait-listed in spite of the fact that Cook's had confirmed the flight by phone that morning. After an hour's wait two seats became available, then half an hour later another. After a strict security check they were on the plane on their way to Kabul.

In Afghanistan they were met by Shaikh Ibrahim's eldest son, Ismail, who took them to the Jamil Hotel where a room with four beds was booked. It looked out onto hills with white houses clinging to the slopes and a 2,500-year-old wall running up the mountain ridges. The air was over 10° C. cooler than Delhi, and the brothers were all relieved to be away from the oppressive heat of India.

When they had settled in they took a taxi to visit Shaikh Ibrahim, who was overjoyed to see Abdullah.

He hugged and kissed him for some minutes then was introduced to Zaid and Abdul. The brothers went to do some prayers then came back to the room where Shaikh Ibrahim was seated on the floor. He told them they would have some food once night fell, then do Maghrib, the evening prayer, before dinner. A young nephew who interpreted prefixed each statement with "My uncle says . . .". At first the Shaikh did not understand what Neil was doing in regard to the fast, and tried to get him to eat. It wasn't until they were having dinner that he fully comprehended. For an Afghan to fast completely would be a very big thing, as they are prodigious eaters. The Shaikh and Ismail, both very big men, kept pressing Zaid and Abdul to eat more. Neil was not upset by the sight of the groaning table and was quite content to drink cold water, although the Shaikh kept asking him to eat at least some fruit. When they left the table they went into a large sitting room with a magnificent carpet on the wall showing the Ka'aba, with rows of people all around. The Shaikh insisted that Abdullah have a small glass of Zam Zam water, then gave one to each other person in the room, ending with himself. The water, which came from the sacred well in the desert, had a strange mineral taste to Neil.

They left early and Neil slept from 9.30 until 2.

Zaid: "An inner attitude operates in me which cannot be bothered with the acquisition of certain kinds of possessions, the things with which people clutter up their houses. If this just sour grapes?"

Abdullah: "To a degree it is sour grapes, because you have no intention of making a permanent home for yourself at present. However, there are other factors working as well. You acquire all the little titbits for your material comfort that take your fancy, so this indicates you are not non-attached to possessions. You are very neat and clean as well as being careful with what you do acquire, so this indicates you must try and see an aspect of insincerity in yourself when you formulate such a question."

Abdul: "What significance do you see in my present illness?" (He was suffering from dysentery with fever.)
Abdullah: "Most illness is brought on by negative emotions of some kind. We would consider this illness to be in that category, the main negative emotions being arrogance, resentment and cavilling. No one can stop a germ coming in, but if you are in a positive state then it doesn't have the same chance of multiplying as when you are negative. When one contracts such a complaint the opportunity is there to learn a great deal about oneself. In your ordinary state of health you have taken on a noisy 'Barry Crump' personality — the tough Kiwi; but once you became sick this departed and you became a whipped cur with such a quiet voice we could hardly hear you speak. This all comes from essence and your identification with the body, which manifests in your ordinary personality or ego as a health crank. What Abdullah is trying to show you is the great need to try to get balance."

Day 13

Neil did not sleep after 2 and the brothers got up for breakfast at about 3, an hour before the gun went off for the start of the day in Ramadhan. Neil felt well and said his prayers with Abdullah at 3.30. Soon after sunrise Abdul started going to the toilet with dysentery, and was laid low. Zaid and Abdullah went to midday prayers at the Pul-i-Khisti or Blue Mosque, which was over 1,000 years old. Both felt there was more fear than love in the congregation so were pleased to get outside and off their haunches after the two-hour session.

They went to Afghan Ariana Airlines to confirm their pre-booked flight to Kandahar, and were told the service had been curtailed through lack of patronage, and they'd have to get a bus like everybody else.

Neil weighed himself and found he had lost 22 lb since arrival in India.

In the evening Zaid and Abdullah went to Shaikh

Ibrahim. Zaid had dinner while Neil sat with cold water, talking to the Shaikh through Sameed. Later the Shaikh spoke about Mecca and the inner attitude toward it from the Naqshibandi point of view, and told Abdullah he was going to give him some inner work to complete his preparations for Mecca. He promised to arrange for the brothers to stay with a friend of his in Mecca.

They were in bed by 9.30, but Neil woke at 11.

Zaid: "Could you please explain a little about the 40-day fast in terms of our particular level of understanding; also can a 40-day spiritual fast be undertaken meaningfully only when a man has reached a level of No. 4?"

Abdullah: "The first part of your question has been answered on Day 2; as to the second, the key word is 'meaningful'. Anyone can do a 40-day fast for whatever purpose they think or need. Very few do it on water alone — most take fruit juice or suchlike as well. You have seen how so many people have asked Abdullah to take this or that liquid. If this fast is to be completed correctly then only water must be taken; there can be nothing added at all. The reason for this is that water is a neutralising force for the body. Impressions, air and water go into the body, and this is how the body is purified physically. The spiritual part of the fast will only be fully realised by the evolution in the scale of man."

Abdul: "It seems that the body is continually pulling all sorts of tricks out of the bag to interfere with the work on oneself. Yet at its own level of intelligence it must be aware of the immense psychological strains that could be imposed on it if the work were to be discontinued. Can you elaborate on this?"

Abdullah: "The body does not want to do this work. Why should it? All it requires is food, warmth, sleep, sex, etc. It is your magnetic centre, which is the seed of the soul, that wants to do the work. There are other things in you which may also want to do the work, such as your centres and essence. The ego and personality may for a while, if they think they can gain greater power, but neither will want to make any real sacrifice or undertake intentional suffering."

Day 14

Neil slept on and off during the night and joined Abdullah with his prayers at 3.30. Neil felt well and was quite relaxed. He wrote for an hour, then he and Zaid went to the airline office to get a refund of their fare to Kandahar, but found it could only be claimed in New Zealand.

Later in the morning, Shaikh Ibrahim sent a car with Sameed to take the brothers to Paghman, several kilometres from Kabul and much higher up the mountains. It was a delightful spot, leafy with poplars and many other trees. A normally rapid-flowing river at this time of the year was just a small creek. They revelled in the cool mountain air, lounging under the trees for several hours.

Back in Kabul, they purchased their bus ticket for Kandahar on Monday. Neil had been on this bus before and was sorry they weren't able to fly, although he had done the trip in summer when the temperature was over 40°C. Zaid and Abdul didn't want to face a dinner at Shaikh Ibrahim's as they were both pretty shaky in the stomach, so decided to have a light fruit meal and mix some powdered milk for a drink.

Neil went to Shaikh Ibrahim's and Abdullah received many instructions on the Naqshibandi way, then returned to the hotel and was asleep by 10.

Zaid: "What is the significance of the Ka'aba at Mecca being in the shape of a cube?"

Abdullah: "Arabic is a cursive language, whereas Latin was in straight lines. The cube is opposite to the flowing lines of Arabic. It is also symbolic of an altar such as was used to make sacrifices to God."

Abdul: "From the degree of questioning you have received from brother Muslims throughout this pilgrimage so far, it seems they are not familiar with fasting as an asceticism, outside the context of Ramadhan. Comparing their lifestyle with the ascetic, controlled existence of the Hindu Swamis and their followers, are the Hindu teachers clearer in their goal of teaching non-attachment to the body and material possessions than their Muslim brothers?"

Abdullah: "It would appear that the mass of the Hindus, compared to the mass of the Muslims, are more controlled with their physical appetites, but we doubt that either is better than the other as far as possessions are concerned. The Hindus, en masse, do not eat with the degree of greed expressed by the Muslims and certainly do not eat anywhere as much in quantity. It must be remembered that we are talking generally, for when we get to the chosen few in both groups who are balanced, there is a similarity in control. The Muslims, being bigger men, may eat more in compensation for their size. The Holy Prophet did not recommend long fasts but suggested one could fast three days a month, controlled by the moon. He understood, however, that a long fast is necessary for some men, but these are few. Knowing his people, he was aware that a long fast was beyond their capabilities. The *Bhagavad-Gita* also teaches this, stressing that the motive for the fast must be pure, otherwise it will build the ego instead of destroying the horror. The final answer to your question is that the Hindus lay a greater stress on non-attachment than their Muslim counterparts."

Day 15

Neil woke at 2.30 and dozed while Abdullah said prayers until 4, then joined Abdullah and said formal prayers. He had further catnaps until 7, when he got up and showered in the uninviting bathroom, a tiny, filthy room containing a toilet, shower, and, in an almost inaccessible recess, hand basin with hot water only. No cold water was available.

Trying to get cool drinking water was a daily problem. The hotel supplied "boiled drinking water" in a teapot, boiling hot, tasting disagreeably of tanin, so Neil had his intake of water at Shaikh Ibrahim's. In spite of the small discomforts Neil was very well.

During the morning he went for a walk with the brothers, and tried to locate parcels sent to them from New Zealand. They had no luck, so left a message with BOAC for Shaikh Ibrahim to be contacted when the parcels arrived. Zaid and Abdul continued trying to find out about the possibility of employment in Afghanistan and Neil went back to the hotel to sort out some of the exercises given him by Shaikh Ibrahim.

At 3 he reported to the Shaikh and was taken to another mosque and shown into a small room. The Shaikh bade him sit down, then proceeded to investigate Abdullah's heart while Abdullah performed one of the exercises. After about half an hour he pronounced it to be "Good, very good. Adam good, Noah and Abraham good, Moses good, Jesus good, Holy Prophet good. Naffs and Temple good — all very, very good." Abdullah and Neil stayed until 8 while Shaikh Ibrahim talked about Islam and asked Neil questions about New Zealand.

Neil went to bed at 10 and slept for four hours.

Zaid: "It seems that the Ka'aba is some kind of pole or force field generator because of the attention directed towards it five times a day all round the world and during Hajj. What is behind this?"

Abdullah: "As you know, everything is vibration, and as such, prayer is on a fine scale. The mass of the prayer will be from fear and reward seeking, so it will be on a coarser vibration than that which is done from love. Taken together, the large quantity of coarse and small of fine that is created at Mecca is the greatest source of fine vibration on the planet. The European Christians understood something of this when in the past they had their altars face the east, the direction of Jerusalem. However, the significance of this has been lost for some time now.

"This fine vibration going up from Mecca helps to

compensate for the very coarse going up from football, racing and these things throughout the world. Unfortunately the Muslim world does most of its suffering in an involuntary way with the exception of Ramadhan, which to a small extent compensates for the rest of the year's misery. To conclude, it would be safe to say that without Mecca and the loyal Muslims around the world we would be in a greater mess than we are now. Also, it shows that the angel who instructed Mohammed saw what was to happen in the future.''

Abdul: ''How and at what stage are the finer energies drawn in during the course of a spiritual discipline like a fast, and would these energies be drawn on by a person consciously doing the Ramadhan fast?''

Abdullah: ''It can be done consciously, although most would create them unconsciously and towards the end of Ramadhan you will see much more tension between people. If people could use this fine energy to remember themselves and God then great benefits would accrue, not only for the people concerned but for the Earth as well.''

Day 16

Neil joined Abdullah with his prayers at 3 and the brothers were up soon after to do their packing. They left the hotel at 5, and although Shaikh Ibrahim had told them they were his guests, the manager made them pay. At the bus depot a continual procession of people thronged past — an interesting cross-section of the ethnic groups that make up Afghanistan.

For the first two hours the bus was cool but the rest of the journey was uncomfortable. There was nobody to meet them when they arrived at Kandahar at noon, so Abdullah decided to send one of the brothers to find their contact. Abdul agreed to go, leaving Zaid and Neil to watch the baggage under the shade of a tarpaulin in front of a melon stall. The heat was intense and the flies even harder to put up with. After a couple of hours' wait, Zaid left Neil to make some enquiries of his own, whereupon Abdul arrived with a van. They loaded it up and proceeded to locate Zaid. Eventually the three were driven to the home of Amunallah, where they were greeted warmly.

They were given a large room with squabs on the floor, unpacked and made themselves comfortable. Neil was very tired so lay down for a rest, after which they broke their fast, Abdul and Zaid having food and Neil water. The brothers went to late prayers which, as it was Ramadhan, consisted of thirty Ra'akats, so Neil told the others in future he wouldn't use up his energy this way. They went to bed about 9.30 and Neil slept until 12.

Abdul: "Judging by the youth of India and Afghanistan, Western materialism is eating away at the traditional religious society. This must inevitably adversely affect the esoteric teaching in the East. Yet in Western consumer society man is becoming more interested in Eastern esoteric teachings, and at the same time becoming wide open to mystic poseurs like the Maharaj Ji. On one side we have potential waning and on the other potential growth. What are your thoughts on this?"

Abdullah: "The key to the question is 'magnetic centre'. As you know, none of us are born with a soul; it is only by our own efforts that we can create one. Roughly half of the population are born with a magnetic centre, which is the seed of the soul. Allah is merciful and a person with no magnetic centre can gain one if he wants it. Usually people without never want one. Many who have a magnetic centre never do anything with it. The ones without are dead, those who do nothing are asleep and those who do work on themselves are awake, as described in the Christian gospels. All that glitters is not gold, so you would find many of the followers of Maharaj Ji in the dead category — these are the people who like the outward show. Obviously many would be sincere and have magnetic centres. To these people Maharaj Ji would be a stepping stone on the way. The road to esotericism is lined with great dangers and many blind alleys, so the pupil must learn to use his intellect as a reconciling force to sort the wheat from the chaff."

Zaid: "Because of the central Islamic teaching of the oneness of God, and the emphasis placed while praying on the Allah O Akbar and the Zikr, after a while a small sense of this oneness seems to seep through. Is this the main reason for our Western participation in this religion?"

Abdullah: "No, it's not the main reason but the second. The main reason is that fundamentally Islam is peace, and teaches the brotherhood of man on this planet. We have to live on the planet to perfect ourselves, and if Islam were practised universally as brotherhood under the fatherhood of God you would have real socialism, from each according to his ability, to each according to his needs. The oneness of God is expounded in the inner teaching of every major religion, for this is a universal truth. We all know the Islamic world does not practise what it preaches, as the wars in Bangladesh and the persecution by Pakistan of the Pakhtun people bear witness. Notwithstanding, Islam is a religion of brotherhood, and a masculine religion among a host of feminine religions."

These eight days were for smell.

Third octave

Day 17

Neil dozed until 2.30 then had a wash. Abdul and Zaid had breakfast at 3.15 and Abdullah decided to take prayers at the same time as the early Muslim prayer, Fajar, about an hour and a half before sunrise, after which they went back to bed until 7. Later in the morning Amunallah brought Shaikh Abdul to see the brothers.

The Shaikh was suffering from Parkinson's disease, and was obviously a very sick man. He looked a lot older to Neil; his old fire had gone and in its place was a wonderful calm. He was overjoyed to see Neil again, and to meet Zaid and Abdul. After a short while he took Neil to an adjoining room where he lay on a bed, asking Abdullah many questions. He told Abdullah that Neil should eat, but when Abdullah explained further he was quite happy, saying only that too much fasting had weakened himself. Later on they all went with the Shaikh to do formal prayers after which they performed some Naqshibandi prayers, using pebbles to count. The Shaikh wanted Abdullah to sit close to him and asked him to put his hands on his legs, which Abdullah did. Abdullah told him he could help him more when he had finished the fast, but the Shaikh said Abdullah had done much as it was.

The two brothers did the last prayer of the night in the mosque. Abdullah and Neil did theirs in the room, to conserve energy. Neil had felt well all day, and that night slept for four hours.

Zaid: "When a Man No. 4 is doing a 40-day fast, does he at any stage have to grapple with malignant forces which may be opposed to his development?"

Abdullah: "Just as there are forces trying to help people with their perfection, there must always be other forces trying to hinder this. If a man is a balanced Man No. 4 then a combination of his own strength and the forces helping him will easily offset the negative qualities arrayed against him. However, the negative forces will then use more subtle tactics, such as trying to direct the fast to the ego, offering many rewards of power. You remember in the Christian Bible story Christ was tempted not with women, but power. The answer, of course, is that all power belongs to God, and whatever attributes a man may gain from any discipline always belong to God. The man is only the channel through which God operates, and if the man forgets this his further progress towards perfection will cease. He will become just one more clever monkey tugged by his desires for power."

Abdul: "What is the process of the soul's evolution from a magnetic centre, and does it usually take a definite time?"

Abdullah: "One may be born with a magnetic centre, depending on the state of being from the previous life, or acquire one by looking for it in this life. If one has a magnetic centre the next step is acquiring a soul, which has to be done by the individual's own efforts of striving against his desires in one way or another. Many people gain this by following the outside teachings of the main religions, a few by trying to understand the inner teachings or esoteric knowledge. To gain a soul can take any time, but the next step of gaining a body kesdjan takes a definite period."

Day 18

The brothers had a very early breakfast so Abdullah and Neil said their prayers at 4.45. Neil had slept better in the coolness of the Kandahar nights, and was physically quite refreshed. He wrote through the morning, attended the midday prayers at the mosque, then walked back to the room, beginning to suffer a little from accumulation of wind.

At 4 the brothers were taken to see Shaikh Abdul, for prayers, then went to another very old mosque in the poorest part of the city where the open sewers gave off terrible smells. Here there were more prayers, followed by a walk through narrow, dusty lanes until they turned into a hole in the wall leading to what appeared to be a subterranean chamber. From here they were shown into a large room straight out of the *Arabian Nights*. Three domes formed the ceiling cum roof, with very small windows set in the masonry; the walls had mirrors inserted everywhere, and shelves containing various bric-a-brac; the floor was covered with carpet over which had been laid a large plastic cover. At the far end was a double bed on a platform.

Shaikh Abdul, who was seated on some cushions in a corner, indicated that he wanted Abdullah to sit close to him. Food was then brought in dishes, and set before the people sitting round the perimeter. It appeared to Neil to be a real feast, and from the enjoyment of the people eating and the comments of Zaid and Abdul, was a delicious meal. They were all concerned because Neil only drank water, and pressed him to take something, which he kept firmly refusing. The Shaikh ate sparingly. Neil held his feet for about an hour, much to the Shaikh's pleasure. After the meal, while the rest were drinking tea, the Shaikh lay on the bed while Neil reclined on the cushions.

Back at the house later that evening, Amunallah asked Abdullah to do some healing. For 21 years an old man had had a headache which Abdullah told him had been caused by negative emotion, and named worry. The old man agreed, after reflection, so Abdullah told him he must pray to Allah that he would be delivered from this worry. Abdullah put his hand on the man's head and prayed to the Holy Healing Force of the Galaxy to cure him; while being silent within he was told the affliction was so deep-seated it would take three sessions to effect a cure.

Neil was asleep by 10.30 and slept for four hours.

Abdul: "Outside the operation of grace, are the periods for the development of a body kesdjan and a mental body pretty much the same?"

Abdullah: "It must always take 21 years to gain a body kesdjan, and it would be possible for a man to be a Man No. 4 at the age of 21. However the majority of men have usually created a lot of negative things in themselves by the time they are 21, so it would be very unusual for a man to become balanced before 40. Hazrat Ali and Vivekananda are two men who come to mind who have become Men No. 4 by the age of 21. The creation of a mental body or Man No. 5 takes 21 years in the majority of cases, often a lot longer. However, it can be done in seven or fourteen years under special circumstances which could be given your name of grace. The creation of a Man No. 6 must take 21 years and this also applies to a Man No. 7, so a little simple arithmetic shows that this is a very difficult task to achieve in a lifetime. The only one who has done this on the planet is the original Zoroaster. The Holy Buddha was a Man No. 6."

Zaid: "Where does irritability come from?"

Abdullah: "Frustration from some part of yourself, mostly the body and ego. Fasting often heightens this, so it provides great opportunity to work on irritability. When Neil first began fasting 21 years ago he invariably became irritable but slowly over the years this diminished. Now you can witness that he is no longer irritable, but accepts everything that happens as being for the best. It is only by struggle against irritability that it will be overcome; then you must put something in its place — acceptance, love or God."

Day 19

Neil joined Abdullah with his prayers at 4.15, then went back to bed till about 7. The brothers sat around talking and writing most of the morning until they were joined by Amunallah, who told them a story of Shaikh Abdul.

A few years previously there had been a bad governor of the province who rounded up all the Mullahs and Shaikhs, putting them into prison without trial. Shaikh Abdul, who was sleeping in the mosque at the time as it was the last ten days of Ramadhan, was put into a cell with only one tiny window above the door. Later in the day he asked if he could perform wuzu so he could pray. The request was refused, but the guard told Amunallah later that he saw the Shaikh outside at midnight washing himself. He reported this to the officer in charge and they inspected the door to find it still locked. The officer told the jailer he himself would keep watch the next night, which he did, and witnessed the Shaikh taking his ablutions outside his cell again. The shaken officer ordered the jailer to leave the cell door open in future.

In the afternoon the brothers moved to a hotel, as the military would not let visitors stay in private houses in Afghanistan. They went to prayers with the Shaikh and retired early. Neil slept from 10 to 2.

Zaid: "When an emotional man has his emotional and moving centres at the same level, what are the symptoms that show the moving centre to be at only a partial stage of development?"

Abdullah: "It doesn't show, because his emotional part will always be a little ahead of the others. The accent will be noticeable in that under duress he will work from his emotional centre to do the work of the other centres, until he has become a balanced man."

Abdul: "The pebbles ritual of the Naqshibandi Sufis we have met in Kandahar has seance-like aspects. What would be the beneficial effects of the ritual?"

Abdullah: "It is a method of remembering God, and as

such must always have a beneficial effect on those taking part. The participants are also remembering other
Naqshibandi saints who are sometimes felt by one or
other of the congregation. Everything depends upon
the growth of the people concerned. Often, of course,
people would get into an emotional state and imagine
they had made this contact, which would hinder their
development.''

Day 20

Today, halfway through the fast, Neil felt very well.
He was not hungry, thus showing that when one fasts
for God one is given other food on a very fine vibration.

The brothers had their breakfast at 3 and Neil joined
Abdullah with his prayers at 4.15. Later in the morning they moved into a better room at the hotel, much to
Zaid's pleasure, as this was the one he had selected
first. They had visits from the Mullah and two friends
who could speak very little English but were able to
convey their concern for Abdullah's health. Amunallah
arrived in the afternoon and Neil told him he would
prefer to meet the Shaikh each day in the morning, at
about 10, to be able to do the midday prayer then go
back to the hotel for a rest in the afternoon. Amunallah
agreed to suggest this to the Shaikh and departed, saying he would be back later that evening. Neil told the
brothers he probably wouldn't, as he was so unreliable,
although Abdullah had yet to give the old man his last
healing session and hoped he would come. They waited
until nearly 11, and when no one came, went to sleep.
Neil woke at 1.

Abdul: "The old man you are channelling the healing
force of Antares into is now being given the opportunity of constructive work on himself. Presumably, if he
fails, the illness resumes. Is the healing one aspect of
grace at work?"

Abdullah: "Yes, it is the grace of God that allows a person to be healed in this fashion. Over a number of years
Neil formulated the idea that one must first eradicate

the cause before curing an ill. Abdullah can work in another way but also subscribes to Neil's ideas on this matter, which is why he told the old man to pray to Allah to become free of worry. The old man will be cured, but if he then continues to worry he will bring the headache back again."

Zaid: "Is the emotional centre dispersed throughout the body more so than the other centres?"

Abdullah: "No, a person may have intellect, emotion or moving qualities in his hands — a good violinist would have the three. Man is the most successful animal on the planet because of his adaptability. A great deal of credit goes to the fact that his centres overlap throughout the body, and when one particular part breaks down, alternative routes can be taken. Thus, if you break your back and have to be in a wheelchair, it does not stop your emotions or intellect working with what is left of your moving centre."

Day 21

Neil slept very little and prayed a great deal all night. He felt well when he arose in the morning. Abdul left for Kabul at 8, and Zaid went out shopping most of the morning, so Abdullah spent the time writing. Neil was expecting Amunallah to take him to see Shaikh Abdul, but waited until 10 that night without word from him. Abdullah told Neil everything happens for the best, and he must not inner consider about Amunallah's lack of consistency. Throughout the afternoon Neil was troubled by a lot of gas in the stomach, so it was perhaps best for him to rest. He did go for a small walk in the evening, and observed that any exertion made him feel tired, which was understandable after 20 days on water alone.

Zaid: "Are the Hindu chakras analogous to the levels of a man's development? Is a man whose energy level is constantly in the fourth chakra a Man No. 4?"

Abdullah: "They are not completely analogous. The chakras relate to a man's development, but the Hindus teach that one can raise them up while meditating only to have them go down again afterwards. In the western world there have been incidents where men who are in charge of boys lead them in a prayer meeting, thus raising the level of their kundalini, then later when it has bounced back down to the sex centre, sexually interfere with the same boys. A balanced Man No. 4 should have love for everyone, thus he would have an attribute of the fourth chakra, but all Men No. 4 are not balanced so there can be a great deal of variation. Really the raising of the kundalini shakati is a continual process that men who are working on themselves go through each day of their lives. In Gurdjieff's words it is using the sex energy to remember yourself, and as Abdullah tells you, to remember God."

Abdul: "Would Gurdjieff have been working with Sufis in the East as a Man No. 4 at the time Rafael Lefort talked of in *The Teachers of Gurdjieff*, or would this have been an initiatory period? Do you think that style of teaching would still go on?"

Abdullah: Abdullah believes that the book you refer to is a lot of hot air, most likely written by someone with their tongue in their cheek. The methods described in the book have been used since Egyptian times, as can be seen by reading *Her Bak*[1]. To those who understand it is obvious Gurdjieff was a Sufi; he received his initiation in the classical way, the same as Neil or any other genuine Naqshibandi. Gurdjieff was also received into other schools and by other teachers. Neil, in a similar way, also experienced this. When a person is on the path to God he will always be led to someone who will be able to take him a step on the way. The Sufis are only one step on this way and Gurdjieff, as well as Neil, was well aware of this. After becoming a Man No. 4, the real teacher must come from within. Among Sufis you will find many Men No. 4 but very seldom a Man No. 5. In proportion the Hindus create more Men No. 5 than any other religion, and the Sufis

[1] *Her Bak,* Vol. I. Isha Schwaller de Lubicz, Hodder and Stoughton, London, 1954.

more Men No. 4. For a man to pass from Man No. 4 to Man No. 5, it is essential for him to find a Man No. 5 to get his baraka. Any development after this comes from above. Inayat Khan is a good example of a man who had to move from the confines of the orthodox Muslim Sufi teaching and imbibe at the fountain of Hindu and other religions. Very few people reading Inayat Khan's books would realise what a wonderfully courageous man he was to be able to blend all these religions in the way he did. To understand this a person would have to live, as we are, among orthodox Muslims and understand something of their bigotry."

Day 22

Neil was troubled with wind and nausea through the night; Abdullah prayed most of the time. Neil decided to cut down on the water intake, as his stomach was shrinking a lot. He had a hot shower when he got up and sat around waiting for Amunallah all day. By 10 in the evening he had not come, nor any word from him. Abdullah told Neil this was a period of waiting which was sent for him to work on patience, forbearance and perseverance.

In the afternoon Zaid and Abdullah were visited by two New Zealanders who were camping in the grounds of the hotel, and had an interesting conversation, although these two were stoned on hashish. Later in the evening when Zaid joined them for a cup of coffee they were apologetic for having visited Abdullah in the state they had been in. When Zaid told Abdullah this he just laughed, saying that if people would only realise the harm they do to themselves with hashish and alcohol they might think twice before indulging too freely. Alcohol brings out the beast in man, while hashish does tend with most to suppress it. However, both are quite artificial experiences, indicating man's mad idea that he can get instant salvation with no real effort. A little of either would not hurt anyone too much, but there are very few people who know how to control themselves, so for the majority it would be better to abstain completely.

Neil went to sleep that night at 10.30 and woke at 2.

Abdul: "With Islam into a conservative decline, what effects do you think this will have on the inner teachings of Sufism?"

Abdullah: "None. Religions have come and gone before this, but the inner teachings, which we call Sufism, have been preserved by people within the religions. The most that happens is that the inner teaching becomes more deeply buried. At the present time in the West it is more on the surface than it has ever been in the past, which bodes well for all mankind. Bigotry and the Police States are the things which will suppress it nowadays, as they have always done in the past."

Zaid: "Is the mental body the same as that called variously by others 'body of light', 'the electronic body' and the 'resurrection body'?"

Abdullah: "No doubt these names convey some idea of what the mental body is. The name mental body itself is inappropriate, just as referring to the higher emotional centre and the higher intellectual centre can lead to misunderstanding at times. These states have nothing to do with emotions and intellect, and many writers of the Gurdjieff system give themselves away by their use and description of so-called contacts with these higher bodies. Gurdjieff himself became a Man No. 5 at the end of his life but none of his followers have done so, from Abdullah's observations of inner knowledge. When Neil has died and the ego has been destroyed, then Abdullah will answer this question more fully. There must be a visit from God for the state of mental body to occur, and without this all is theory."

Day 23

Neil had a good night's sleep, dozing from 2 until 4, when he joined Abdullah in prayers.

The hotel was so full it was impossible to get into the

toilet or shower until 10. The Afghan hotels had not impressed the brothers. There were no single rooms at all, most having from three to five beds, and no place to hang anything — Zaid put up lines from a window to any point he could fix a nail to. When they moved into the present room they'd found the servant making up the beds without changing the linen. At the last hotel there had been only one sheet so at least it was an improvement to have two. The hotels were unbelievably noisy, with doors slamming, radios blaring, people shouting until nearly midnight. The previous night had been particularly busy as there was a bus load of tourists from Europe, several VW Kombis and about twenty people in the rooms of the hotel. Travellers were sleeping on verandahs and anywhere else they could find to doss down. One of the hotel's two toilets was next-door to the brothers' room, and was well patronised all night. As Abdullah told Zaid, all these conditions were for some purpose and must be accepted with equanimity.

Amunallah arrived mid morning saying he had sent someone with a message to the Shaikh, who was going to contact the hotel at 11. They waited until 12.25, when Abdullah suggested they go to the mosque and see the Shaikh themselves.

The Shaikh was pleased to see Abdullah, kissed him and Zaid warmly, and said he was happy with Abdullah's suggestions about meeting each morning. Amunallah reported that the police were worrying the hotel staff about the brothers' movements and wanted a report on their comings and goings each day, so Abdullah said he should let them know the visit was spiritual, having nothing to do with politics. Amunallah promised to do this, but the brothers had reservations about his ability to carry out what he said. However, realising that everything comes from Allah, they were quite resigned to whatever might happen. Returning to the hotel, they spent the rest of the day reading and writing until they went to sleep at 10.30. Neil woke at 12.

Zaid: "When you tell us 'It is the Teaching that matters rather than the teacher', does this mean that the Teaching is not only a force coming from God, but perhaps a higher part of God Himself?"

Abdullah: "It is a force coming from God, so in this solar system is one of the three forces of our Holy Father the Sun. Hazrat Inayat Khan says it is the Spirit of Guidance, which to Abdullah is a very good description. The force is an aspect of the Holy Neutralising Force of the Sun — in the Christian Bible, the Holy Ghost. We can also contact it on another level from the Holy Active Force of the Sun, as our conscience within."

Abdul: "Gurdjieff's sex life appears erratic, from what we read. What is your opinion?"

Abdullah: "Sex was one of Gurdjieff's stumbling blocks; although he knew more than most men about the use of sex energy he was dominated by it for many years. He would have become a Man No. 5 years before he did had he been able to control his sexual drive more adequately. By this Abdullah is not implying that it completely ruled him, but rather that he had so much sex energy it took a great deal more fine energy for him to keep it contained. He should have used it for the birth of his mental body. He did some pretty shabby things because of this sexual drive, and although we concede he did some consciously, some others were examples of identification, for which he had to pay."

Day 24

Neil slept on and off until 3, when Zaid had his breakfast and did his prayers. Neil joined Abdullah in prayers, then they rested until 8. The morning was pleasingly cool. Amunallah didn't come all day, so Neil was confined to the hotel. He was feeling the effects of phlegm in his windpipe, and as he couldn't drink through the day to wash it down, soon developed indigestion, which, combined with wind, made him fairly uncomfortable all day. In the afternoon he and Zaid went for a walk to a nearby park, then found a shady spot near the hotel to spend a few hours. They went to bed at 10.30 and Neil slept until 2.

Zaid: "For a newly converted Muslim, what is the point of making a pilgrimage to Mecca?"

Abdullah: "There is no difference in this need for a new or an old Muslim; it is one of the acts of faith as a Muslim. Also, for a Sufi like yourself it means you have completed an octave which is very important for your spiritual growth. You remember what was said in relation to the vibration given up from Mecca with all the practising Muslims facing there at least once a day, so you will also realise how valuable it will be for you to go to that Holy Force on the planet. There is no other place like it on this planet today, and not-withstanding the ignorance of so many Muslims it is a beacon in the darkness of materialism. Without Mecca the world would be a very black place indeed."

Abdul: "Why is it that so many Muslims we have met are so bigoted?"

Abdullah: "Islam was a rallying cry for the people of the desert to give up their evil ways of drunkenness and idolatry. The Holy Prophet had a very illiterate rabble to deal with and the strongest weapon he could use was fear, reward and punishment, so this is what he concentrated on. As can be seen from history it was very effective, for in less than a hundred years Islam was challenging the known world of the day. Because of the Law of Seven, anything based on fear, reward and punishment must contain the seeds of its own destruction, and that is what you are seeing with those who persist in talking about the religion on the surface instead of seeing deeper to the truth within."

These eight days were for touch.

Fourth octave

Day 25

Neil had very little sleep after 2, feeling sick in the stomach with wind and indigestion because of the bile coming up and going down continuously whenever he was asleep. He was in good spirits, knowing that this was all a part of his voluntary suffering created by the fast, and realising that this action of the body was part of the cleansing process, indicating that the instinctive centre was working normally. Neil marvelled at the intelligence of the body in the way it was taking care of the purifying process so that when the forty days were up he would indeed be like a newborn child, free from all impurities.

Amunallah called at 11 with fruit and apologies for not coming the day before. He took Neil to the Shaikh's house and left him. Neil was received in a long narrow room on the top floor, which led to a small bedroom occupied by the Shaikh. They sat for a while, then the Shaikh went into the bedroom and Neil was joined by a young boy, followed by three men. The Shaikh came back, talked to the people, then disappeared again. This went on until all adjourned to the mosque for midday prayers, after which Neil went back to the hotel to spend the afternoon writing. He went to sleep at 9.30 and woke at 1.

Zaid: "How can a pupil serve his teacher when separated from him?"

Abdullah: "The best example is that given previously about the two people who were pupils of Hazrat Inayat Khan. The teacher gives the pupil certain tasks which, if carried out faithfully, will greatly assist the pupil on the path of his own perfection. If the pupil prays for his teacher each day then this will be the best way he can repay the teacher's efforts on his behalf. After all, it is God who does everything through us; He is both the Knower and the Known, thus pupil and teacher are the same, being just different aspects of the One."

Abdul: "There is an obvious problem in guidance when one's teacher is not available, yet one knows that the guidance is internally available. The pendulum or dowsing is one technique you have shown us for contacting the higher self. Are there any others?"

Abdullah: "Yes, the other method is to learn to become silent. One must learn to be able to completely still the associative thinking that is going on continuously in the mind. This is the same as going into samadhi with seed which Yogis practise, and has other names such as contemplation, meditation, etc. It is perhaps the most difficult of all these disciplines. Abdullah suggests you try to do it properly for a minute a day until this is nearly possible, then increase by a minute until you can do it for about twenty minutes. This will take several years. Sometimes we are told by pupils that they can do this, when we know it is all in their imagination."

Day 26

It was a very noisy night and Neil had less sleep than usual. There were a number of Pakistani travellers staying at the hotel who appeared never to have been taught any consideration for others. The children ran wild, making a terrible noise, with never a word from the parents who themselves shouted, slammed doors, and generally disregarded everyone else in the place. Their toilet habits particularly were trying to Neil, resting uneasily on the other side of the wall.

This type of "Asian toilet", as the brothers called it, consisted of a shaped slab of porcelain inset into concrete with slightly raised places for the feet. The designers must have supposed the users would know something about hygiene, which was, however, lamentably lacking. A pipe went down to a chamber about 12" below the ground, which obviously was never cleaned, and the smell from the coating of excreta was sheer hell for Neil on his empty stomach so he always went armed with a handkerchief over his nose. All night, Bang! — the screen door, then BANG! the inside door; scuffle around the bathroom, followed by a tremendous roar echoing down the pipe into a miniature thunderstorm, and a loud lapping of water on the bottom. About every third person would play the anvil chorus on the cistern, which usually was empty; the others didn't bother to try. After each onslaught Neil would withdraw his nose under the bedclothes as the stench seeped through the slack door.

In the morning, Neil went and sat with Shaikh Abdul, saying midday prayers with him, then returned to the hotel in the afternoon to write. He and Zaid went to bed early and Neil slept from 9.30 to 1.

Zaid: "When a teacher becomes a Man No. 5 there must also be a change in the relationship between teacher and pupil. Does this come from the teacher only, or must the pupil contribute something? Should the pupil try to work in a different way?"

Abdullah: "The teacher's progress is different from the pupil's because the pupil is still unbalanced while the teacher is balanced. If the pupil has discernment he will be able to sense, think or feel this, depending on his state of development, consequently his attitude towards his teacher must change. As Ramana Maharshi said, 'We don't grow horns', so it is up to the pupil to recognise the teacher from his own growth. The pupil continues to work in the way the teacher indicates, no matter what the teacher's development."

Abdul: "It seems that even when one becomes a Man

No. 5, like Shaikh Abdul, one may still not have sufficient breadth of vision to see through the outer forms
of things, e.g. his criticism of long fingernails and close
adherence to the other outer forms of Islam. Could you
comment?"

Abdullah: "A person on a lower scale of development
often finds the actions of those who are more
developed inexplicable. The Shaikh works within his
own environment, which Allah has placed him in. He is
not so concerned with the temporal affairs of people
but with their spiritual development, so using the
Islamic religion he guides them to further perfection.
He would be aware, as you are, of the stagnation of the
life they live outwardly but within the framework in
which he is placed he is working for them consciously."

Day 27

Neil was awake most of the night but had a short sleep
from about 4.30 till 6. He was feeling well except for
the nausea which often caused him some distress. He
decided, on advice from his guide, to cut his water intake down to four glasses, as it was after a drink that
he experienced most discomfort. He decided not to go
to the mosque, as the Friday service would take a long
time, but in the afternoon he and Zaid went for a walk.
He was very tired when he got back, so lay on the bed
until going to sleep at 9.30. He awoke at 1.

Abdul: "The 40-day fast is already a hard discipline. It
seems some of the trouble with phlegm and dry mouth
could simply be cleared up by breaking Ramadhan and
taking the odd drink of water during the day."

Abdullah: "Why do you think Neil was sent to Kandahar to do this fast? Wouldn't it have been physically
much easier at home with a loving wife and children?
For Neil to do this fast drinking when he pleased and
under favourable conditions, was not intended by
Allah. That is why we were sent to Muniji's ashram,
where one day would be equal to a week of fasting in
normal circumstances. Allah knows!"

Zaid: "We know Shaikh Abdul to be a very saintly person and a Man No. 5. He appears to have always worked within the framework of Islam and it is puzzling why there is no group nor school around him which aims to give the truth of the Teaching to as many as possible."

Abdullah: "How do you know this? Abdullah is sure he has an inner circle because he has been in it. However, the Shaikh works mostly with the ignorant people, so he cuts his cloth accordingly. As Abdullah said in answer to Abdul's question on Day 26, the actions of a Man No. 5 cannot readily be understood by people on a lower level. Remember what was said by Hermes Trismegistus — 'As above, so below'; but what is understood above is often incomprehensible to those below. The great hope for those below is that this knowledge is contained in themselves, and if they will work on raising their vibrations it will become available."

Day 28

Neil lay awake most of the night, saying prayers until after Zaid had had his breakfast. At about 5 he went to sleep for a short time and had this dream:

He was coming from the Three Lamps in Ponsonby to the city, hurrying to catch a tram (trams had not been running for over 10 years). By running he just managed to get the tram, getting off at Victoria Park where he walked across toward a firm who made nails. When he arrived at the factory he stopped in the yard where two people were putting a straw man on a cross and telling a puppet-like brown man that they were crucifying him. Neil told them not to say this, as he would think it was true, to which they laughingly replied that it would not matter as he already believed it anyway. The next thing Neil became aware of was that on the way to the factory he had eaten a tomato while asleep. This caused him great distress as he knew he had not finished his fast, and he tried to get the bits of skin out of his mouth. He decided he would have to confess he had broken the fast, however much it hurt him. After this he found he was under the cross which was covered by a steel cage and weighed heavily upon him, causing great agony. Neil appealed to the two men to lift it off and although they tried, they found it too heavy. Neil then cried out for some other men to come and help, which they did, allowing him to clamber out still trying to spit the tomato skins out of his mouth. This was an esoteric dream which Abdullah leaves to the reader to work out for himself.

Neil saw Shaikh Abdul as usual, and did the midday prayers with him. He went to sleep at 10, for four hours. Abdul arrived back from Kabul.

Zaid: "Why did the Prophet of Islam ask his followers to keep the fast of Ramadhan?"

Abdullah: "It was an instruction from above, revealed in the Koran. The fast of Ramadhan was an ancient Jewish fast also, and some of the revelations to the Prophet occurred in this month. He understood his people well, and realising their limitations and the harshness of the climate, thought this would be the most suitable type of fast to impose on them."

Abdul: " 'To him who has much been given, much shall be expected', says the Bible. Is this the reason why the man set on a course of conscious soul development can expect greater and more severe tests as he progresses on the way?"

Abdullah: "Yes, as one develops then many things become harder, mainly because one becomes more aware of one's shortcomings. This is why it is dangerous to wake a person up too early. It's far better for the person to awaken at his own pace."

Day 29

Neil slept for about two hours after prayers. He was suffering badly from phlegm and vomited when he woke up because the phlegm persisted in blocking his throat. He understood that this was all a part of the cleansing of the body, accepting it philosophically.

Later in the morning he visited Shaikh Abdul, they did their usual Naqshibandi exercise followed by formal prayers in the mosque, and the rest of the day was spent writing and resting at the hotel. He slept from 10 until 1.

Zaid: "In one of his books[1] Gurdjieff describes and locates the three brains, or centres, in the human body. He describes the brain which manifests the third force, the reconciling force, as being localised in the solar plexus, but also as being a mass of separate concentrations scattered throughout the body. This seems contrary to Abdullah's teaching — could you please explain?"

Abdullah: "Abdullah believes that the difference between man and woman, other than the obvious physiological difference, is the way they react in the three brains. To Abdullah, a man initiates with his moving brain, denies with his emotions and reconciles with his intellect. A woman initiates with her emotions, denies with her moving centre and also reconciles with her intellect. On the surface this would appear to be completely different from what Gurdjieff says; however, the key to understanding it is the fact that all these brains overlap, thus although a man may initiate with his moving centre, in many cases it is with the intellect of the moving centre, so as this is also connected to the intellectual centre, there is no real difference."

Abdul: "At what stage in one's development does one's guide stop being the neutral observer?"

Abdullah: "When one gains a body kesdjan. You can contact your guide before this, but he or she will only answer your questions, thus you have to do all the initiating; the guide still remains passive."

[1] *All and Everything,* G.I. Gurdjieff, Routledge & Kegan Paul, London.

Day 30

Neil dozed until 6 after doing his prayers at 3.30. This morning they were going to see the police with Amunallah, to have their visas extended, but about 11 Amunallah rang to say he would come the next day instead. Abdullah decided to go to the Shaikh and Abdul went with him. In the afternoon Neil was still having trouble with phlegm so he went to bed at 7 and slept from 9.30 till 12.

Zaid: "During the last two weeks in Kandahar it has been necessary to try to work positively against the effects of boredom, and to accept the situation of waiting. Is this position a specific lesson that we have to learn?"

Abdullah: "The Holy Prophet said that among the main things needed on the esoteric path are patience and perseverance. This is what we have to summon up in ourselves in the situation we find operating here. All progress necessitates waiting in a humble fashion for the results of our actions, whether good or bad."

Abdul: "What factors determine the part the guide plays in a developmental triad? Can you say something about these triads?"

Abdullan: "There are many triads formed in man. The lower ones and some of the higher have been covered in *Probings.* As you have been asking about the kesdjan body, the triad you are looking for is: Chris is your three brains, Abdul is your spiritual part and your guide is the third part. Abdul in this triad would be your body kesdjan, if you had one. However, he is still either your magnetic centre or soul, depending on your development."

Day 31

Neil had hardly any sleep or rest through the night as the phlegm caused much distress. He got up early and had a shower, hoping to shift it by moving about; however, it persisted all day. The brothers waited all morning for Amunallah to take them to the police, but as usual he let them down, so they went on their own. After two hours at the station they at last learned that if they came back the day before their visas expired they would be renewed. Neil returned to the hotel very tired, and while resting had a visit from Amunallah, apologetic as usual, who repeated the information about the visas. Neil went to sleep at 11 and woke at 2.30.

Abdul: "Apart from its obvious time-keeping functions in Ramadhan, what esoteric part does the moon play?"

Abdullah: "The moon, like the earth, when shining in space is a reflection of the Sun. The esoteric function of the moon is to show how everything feeds on something else and if not, must do as Neil's body is doing on the fast, feed on itself. As you have been able to witness, this necessitates conscious suffering."

Zaid: "At the pupil's level of development, what are the effects of a fast over several days, apart from working against the body?"

Abdullah: "It all depends on the degree of development. All fasts must help to make the body obedient, but they won't necessarily have the same effect spiritually for everyone. The key is motive. If you have the correct motive for the fast, then in the end the correct result will accrue. Many people do fasts out of vanity, pride, etc. and as such these fasts only build the ego. The attitude to adopt, at first intellectually or emotionally, then spiritually, is that the fast is for God."

Day 32

Neil slept on and off after prayers until 6, feeling fairly sick in the stomach. Later he and Zaid went to a bank to cash some traveller's cheques and were redirected to the State Bank, where it took over two hours to transact their business. Waiting in any place like this was always rewarding, as one saw a cross section of the moving public. There were many Europeans waiting, and Neil sat opposite a French hippy suffering from drug withdrawal who was in such bad shape that his friend had to do everything for him, and when the money came through led him to the counter and out the door to further degradation.

When Neil arrived back at the hotel he lay down feeling sick and tired, remaining thus all day. He went to bed early, getting to sleep at 10 and awaking at 12.

Zaid: "In *All and Everything* Gurdjieff mentions again and again something which he calls 'being-Partkdolg-duty'. This brings to mind the idea of needing to repay in some way for the arising of one's existence. How does this work?"

Abdullah: " 'Being-Partkdolg-duty' is your conscious labours and intentional suffering indicating that to pay for one's arising one must voluntarily suffer, working on oneself in as conscious a way as possible. The fasts you and Abdul are doing on the intervals of Abdullah's complete octaves are one way. The other way for you is not to get upset and judge all these people around you, but rather try to forgive them in their ignorance."

Abdul: "I've always been intrigued by the strong pull England has for me, which I don't think is explained by the fact of having relatives there. The little theme 'Oranges and Lemons' that the BBC plays on the Eastern service evokes this attraction. Would its roots lie in deep essence?"

Abdullah: "The call would come mainly from your essence, although if your people spoke about the old country with attachment then it would also be in your personality or ego. Nationalism is something that is engendered in a person by years and years of brainwashing, but the attraction of climatic conditions would be from the essence of the particular race after centuries of living in such places."

These eight days were for sight.

Fifth octave

Day 33

Neil was awake until after 4.30 when he vomited some bile, which cleared his throat, allowing him to go into a short sleep. He had the following dream:

He was in bed at home with his wife when he heard sounds, so got up to find his daughter Jeannine in the kitchen, which was bathed in a tremendous white light. Jeannine, aged about eight or nine years, was slim in a white nightie which was shining vividly. A stove was on, with a baking dish on top, in front of which was one egg in the shell. Jeannine said she was getting the breakfast, and Neil told her it was an hour too early. She began to cry and Neil comforted her, leading her back to bed. The dream continued with Neil and his wife in the kitchen about to serve the breakfast an hour later. A friend, Trevor, arrived with three loaves of bread, accompanied by a shadow Trevor also with three loaves. Neil paid them both and explained that he was in a hurry, at which Trevor became angry, saying Neil was always in a hurry when he called. Neil pacified them and led them out, saying it was a bit early to give them some wine. They went away muttering.

Neil and Zaid went later to Shaikh Abdul, returning to the hotel with Neil still feeling sick. He went to bed early and had very little sleep.

Abdul: "Does the development of the three main centres influence the soul?"

Abdullah: "Not necessarily. There would be hundreds of people very under-developed in their centres who have souls, as well as many with a high degree of development in their centres who have no soul. The main object in balancing and developing the three brains in a spiritual way is to create, eventually, a balanced body kesdjan."

Zaid: "When praying at regular times, certain set forms and prayers are usually used, but one finds that more spontaneous prayers made on the spot and said from the heart seem to be more sincere. What is the correct way?"

Abdullah: "It depends upon the individual. Some people have no capacity for formulating prayers, so for them formal prayers would be better than none at all. For those who can formulate their prayers, then those from the heart are more genuine. The major problem that arises from this type of prayer is that often the devotional aspect gives way to asking for rewards."

Day 34

The brothers endured a very noisy night with little sleep, as a large number of Pakistanis was in residence. Neil was experiencing a great deal of pain in the stomach from bile and wind. He couldn't drink much water, because it just stopped in the top stomach with a small amount going through the bladder and none getting into the lower, as he found when he gave himself an enema. He decided not to go to the main midday prayers as they took too long, but went for a short walk, then rested until going to bed. He went to sleep at 9.30 and awoke at 2.

Zaid: "In Abdullah's prayers, Jalal al-Din Rumi receives an important place at the head of a list of teachers and is referred to as 'beloved Caliph'. Could you please explain this?"

Abdullah: "Rumi was a Man No. 5 when he died and later became a Man No. 6, so he thus materialised as one of the top men of the planet. Because of this degree of development he became the head of the Sufis under Hazrat Ali, who also has other bigger tasks to perform.''

Abdul: "Our joining in the 40-day fast in the last eight days provides a vibration which can presumably help you if we have the right attitude, service without reward. Could one similarly hope, by directing a fast towards one's parents or friends, to help them during a difficult period?''

Abdullah: "Remember what you have just said, 'service without seeking rewards'. It is only by God's grace that your voluntary suffering will help anyone. We must not expect anything, but rather dedicate our efforts to some person then leave it to God to decide whether the person deserves help or not.''

Day 35

A quiet night, so Neil slept more than the previous one; however, he suffered a great deal with pain, feeling very sick. He and Abdul went to see the Shaikh and attended midday prayers, then came back to the hotel where Neil rested until going to sleep at 10. He woke at 2.

Zaid: "The eight-day fast currently in progress started off in a negative fashion. Is this particular kind of negativity a form of denying characteristic of an emotional man?''

Abdullah: "It can happen this way to any type of man, 1, 2 or 3, because a fast goes against the body and this kicks back always in one way or another. We all make patterns of behaviour while growing up, and when we strike this work find that they cloud all our efforts. You have in you what Neil called 'Black Denis', so when you make a big effort as you are doing now, this moody part takes over if you don't fight him constantly.''

Abdul: "Where does curiosity end and genuine spiritual questioning begin? Some bigger questions relating to the way one should direct one's life, job,

marriage, etc. often seem cases for major spiritual
direction, particularly when one has doubts as to the
extent that one should try to 'hobble the camel'."

Abdullah: "Curiosity can be genuine when objective,
but most is quite subjective, so of no value on the
spiritual path. Abdullah considers it to be a womanish
characteristic, and has observed over the years that
men who are subjectively curious are usually 'old
women'. When you dig into the real part of yourself
you must find that all you are doing in life has in some
way a connection with your spiritual development,
therefore when you get into the real part of yourself
the right questions will arise."

Day 36

Neil didn't sleep after 2. Abdullah fruitfully spent the
time praying while Neil was sick with phlegm. It was
now a constant stream, aggravated by having to lie on
his back. When he tried to lie on his side he found his
lungs became more or less collapsed, along with his
stomach. He had begun to feel dizzy when he stood up,
so decided not to go to the mosque, but was able to do
some writing. He went to bed at 8 and slept from 10.30
till 2.

Abdul: "You have mentioned the case of a couple in the
U.S.A. who carried out a spiritual task Hazrat Inayat
Khan had given them so that years later he was able to
guide them to the next stage. There are people who
find it difficult to sell up house, leave their jobs, etc. to
go to a teacher who may be some distance away, yet we
know a teacher is necessary. How close and constant
does the connection need to be between teacher and
pupil?"

Abdullah: "Allah knows! Wherever you find the work
is the right place for you to start your struggle. The
Sufi teaching pre-supposes a person will have a teacher
because this is the way they usually operate; however,
for some time a person's teacher may be books, or delv-
ing into the esoteric side of their ordinary religion.

When the pupil is ready he will find his teacher, because God will lead them to each other."

Zaid: "A Man No. 5 is apparently on the fifth step of the octave of his development. In the musical scale of vibration this step is named for Sol, the Sun. Is this of any significance?"

Abdullah: "When a man becomes a Man No. 5 he is assured that at the death of his mortal body he will in spirit go to the Sun, thus he has acquired in himself a sympathetic vibration with the lowest level of the Sun. As the tonic Solfah came from an esoteric school, they were most likely well aware of this fact when they put Sol in at this point."

Day 37

Neil dozed a bit after 4.30. He observed the first gurgles in his intestines for over a month, and supposed that the bile must be beginning to move at last. He felt better, although fairly out of sorts, and for the first time in a few weeks enjoyed a drink of water.

He and the brothers went to the police to get an extension of their visas, which took several hours. He had a reasonable day and kept on his feet for a long time, although he had spasms of dizziness. Amunallah arrived in the afternoon with some petrol for the stove and a selection of dried fruit. Neil weighed himself and found he had lost 36 lb in the last 24 days. Abdul and Zaid were both feeling tired, as this was their fifth day of fasting on water alone.

Abdul: "In the little book published by Ramdas's Anandashram, *Thus Speaks Ramdas,* one notes Ramdas saying ' . . . get inspiration from saints but do not think of taking shelter permanently in any ashram.' This bears again on the question of the need for an external guide or teacher in the life of those following one of the ways. Could you comment?"

Abdullah: "What Ramdas is saying here is that it is good to visit saints, taking their darshan, or baraka. This is a way of devotion, but the pupil is always relying upon the teacher's presence, which makes him very dependent. It is necessary at times to have this contact, but it can become a hindrance if the pupil will not let go and learn to depend upon his own efforts and his teacher within himself."

Zaid: "I am puzzled about the division of Abdullah's fast into five groups of octaves of eight days. In the usual sequence of octaves of vibration the upper Do becomes the lower Do of the next octave, so that the units of frequency appear to proceed in sevens. With the 40-day fast, each octave succeeds the previous instead of overlapping, so that each octave starts on a different day or frequency number. Why is this so? It appears to create a portion of inner octave which begins on Do and ends on the fifth note, Sol."

Abdullah: "It is related to the Law of Ninefoldness which is three complete triads. Abdullah explained in answer to Abdul's question on Day 2 about the Law of Seven in relation to the fast. What you now have to do is understand the Law of Ninefoldness in relation to the fast."

Day 38

Neil didn't sleep all night, as he was violently vomiting and suffering with his empty stomach and phlegm. After 5 he managed to get an hour's sleep, waking up quite refreshed. He went to the Shaikh for an hour and a half, then back to the hotel to rest. He was very sick again in the evening, and after going to sleep at 11 was wakened at 12 by gunfire announcing the end of Ramadhan. The brothers had started Ramadhan in India, where it was expected to finish on October 18. The Afghanis expected it might finish on October 17 but ended it a day earlier on a radio report from Arabia.

Abdul: "Mankind seems to get really side-tracked in striving for perfection — the urge to travel, climb mountains, find the ideal woman, even to perfectly restore a vintage car, all seem to be expressions of the same inner striving. What is your comment on this?"

Abdullah: "It is part of man's birthright to strive for perfection, but because of his identification with the body and sense objects, much of this striving must be directed to subjective perfection. This helps him to build up his ego by becoming the top climber or whatever, and the goal of objective perfection is lost."

Zaid: "If fasts are not undertaken regularly, can the body win back its strength and domination?"

Abdullah: "The body does not have to be strong in health to dominate the man — often the contrary. Your body has been feeling weak and lethargic for several days now, yet has clouded all your thinking. If a person practises fasting for some years, as Neil did, then of course he gains the strength to be able to control the body under all conditions, making it passive and obedient."

Day 39

Neil lay awake for a long time after the guns, then dozed for an hour until 4, when he joined Abdullah with his prayers. Shaikh Abdul sent his servant with some milk at about 6.30 and Abdullah told Zaid and Abdul they must break their fast so as to protect him during the completion of his 40 days. This they agreed to do, so they all went through the act of boiling the milk and the two brothers began eating. Neil agreed to drink through the day so they boiled him some water, which he drank hot. He was very sick in the afternoon but had a better night, sleeping from 9.30 until 1.

Zaid: "In the spiritual sense, what is the most important thing we should have learned from the Afghanistan experiences?"

Abdullah: "Your limitations. You must be able to assess what you have done in the past and reconcile it with what you are doing in these circumstances."

Abdul: "The passage of time has taken on much more significance to me during Abdullah and Neil's fast. Is this a taste of real self-remembering?"

Abdullah: "It could well be, if it has some connotation

of God at the back of it. 'The ever present here and the eternal now' are names of God, and if remembered as such form a part of real self-remembering. The fast obviously acts as a shock on all those who come in contact with it, even if they push it down immediately by self-calming in one way or another. An act of conscious suffering can never be ignored completely, although, like one's conscience, it can quite readily be pushed down and buried to let the observer go back to sleep again quickly.''

Day 40

Neil was awake from 1 until after 6, then had half an hour's sleep. He was feeling much better in the stomach, although very dizzy, so went out on the verandah and sat in the sun for an hour. He was sick all day, but quite cheerful, as he knew the end was in sight. To complete the 40 days required only the night's fast, and by now he was not concerned about lying awake all night. At 9 Neil went to sleep for one hour, then lay awake until after 11 when, for the first time in over 40 days, he literally died until after 6 o'clock . . .

Abdullah awoke, remembering farewells from Neil and his shadowy ego, to hear in his inner ear a voice calling "Abdullah! Abdullah!" The body felt very refreshed after such a long sleep, taking hot water until 9, when Abdullah made himself a hot drink with milk powder and glucose, thus breaking the fast of 40 days and 40 nights on water alone.

Zaid: "What is the result of the three travellers living together for two months through all sorts of trying conditions?"

Abdullah: "Each will benefit according to his real inner development on a personal scale. All should have learned about external considering and the state of tolerance they possess. There should now be a real feeling of love between all, without judgement on anyone's part, and an eager desire to help one another with the advancement of their spiritual development."

Abdul: "Abdullah's conscious efforts and voluntary sufferings during this 40-day fast seem to give a sense of proportion to ordinary man's position on the scale of vibration from His Endlessness. It seems that we have to become conscious beings just to be noticed."

Abdullah: "As is said in the Christian Bible, not even the death of a sparrow goes unnoticed, but in relation to His Endlessness this is on a different scale. Mankind has God within, in the form of conscience, so everything a person does is observed and recorded in his own subconscious mind, and certain things are taken from life to life in this manner. We doubt that even on the scale of Man No. 7 we would warrant any recognition above that of Ahura Mazda. What we have to do is learn to serve, to the best of our ability, all above and our fellow men below, in modest stillness and humility."

These last eight days were for hearing.

Learning patience

Abdullah began breaking the fast by taking a glass of powdered milk, then at intervals through the day small quantities of jelly, arrowroot, liquid instant breakfast, and a piece of watermelon, the only solid. He went to sleep at 10 p.m. and woke an hour later with his lungs in great distress, but after coughing a lot went back to sleep until morning. For breakfast he had blancmange cooked with raisins and jelly, later some Milo and cake, then for lunch cooked a soup with chicken left from the brothers' lunch, marrow, onions, apple, powdered soup and soya beans.

In the afternoon he went to the Post Office to make a toll call to his wife; Abdul had tried for the two previous days, without success. The Afghan postal services left much to be desired, as the employees, like the majority of Afghans, were preoccupied with supplementing their small wages with baksheesh. Even when selling stamps they asked for a kick-back. The previous time Neil had been in Afghanistan his wife had received only two of more than twenty letters because, as he was later told, the staff would remove the stamps for resale. This time he had been buying letter cards which had the stamps printed on. If he sent a letter he registered it and made the clerk frank it in front of him.

After six hours the call was made. Although he had to pay for three minutes before they would make any reservations for him, he was charged more money for an extra two minutes because of a misunderstanding between Paris and Kabul. The connection was so bad he could hear only an odd word, but his wife told him she could hear his voice well. For all this he had to pay $US31. As he told Abdul, Allah was certainly teaching him plenty about tolerance.

Abdullah's body recovered in a couple of days and he was able to go to the mosque where he prayed with Shaikh Abdul. On the fifth night after breaking the fast he suffered much discomfort so decided to cut down on the intake of food, as it was not being digested but passing through his body whole. After this he had no further trouble, and the body put on condition at an amazing rate.

Zaid had been worried about his own loss of weight so Abdullah explained to him that his negative emotion, especially resentment and judging of the native population, was poisoning his whole system. Abdullah conceded that Zaid had picked up a bug but told him it would go in a few days if Zaid would stop worrying about himself; however this was beyond Zaid's capabilities, and following an old pattern, he decided to run away. Four days after the end of the fast he left for London, and Abdullah received a note from him written two weeks later, saying Zaid was in a London hospital. Abdullah had a feeling of love for Zaid and was sorry he couldn't keep going, thus curing himself, as Abdullah was sure the bug had been fed by Zaid's negative state.

Because of the identification with the body as being the self, all three types of men — moving, emotional, and intellectual — mollycoddle the body instead of realising that whatever happens is only the result of some previous action. Because Neil had been wounded in the Second World War, Abdullah would have to put up with aches of the body, and indeed Neil had learned to do this, using all sickness as the way of the Fakir, to destroy the identification with the body as being the self. There is no easy way to do this. It must be done through the agony of the body, along with great struggle against self-calming. In these days people are conditioned to be spectators — they want someone else to do the suffering. This is why the idea that "Christ died for you" is so popular. As Gurdjieff said, this earth is a pain factory, so most must suffer at one time or another. If you accept it in a positive way you will make some being for yourself, but if you cringe from it, as most do, then be prepared to pay the price. People are always able to find some justification for their actions pertaining to their bodies, but this is just self-calming and cuts no ice on the spiritual scale.

Everything is God; thus a cancer cell is God, along with all the other bugs and viruses delineated by man. If you get a cold, usually you will find you have been negative; if you don't find negativity, then you most likely have a buffer about this particular negative emotion in yourself. You will have been negative, make no mistake about it! The next thing is to accept that you have been negative and that you are host to the bug. Under these circumstances Neil would let the bug alone for three days to give it its chance of life, then if the cold had not gone away in this period he would take some relief. This had not been necessary for some years. Obviously if one gets cancer or some other similar disease then something drastic has to be done. Man's chance as well as the cancer's exists only while there is life, so to protect the planetary body one has an operation to remove the cancer or takes other remedial action. In extreme old age the patient may decide that the bug may have the body, as the Spirit's work with the body is finished. Ramana Maharshi acted in this fashion, although he wasn't very old.

As the days passed Abdullah began to experience further spiritual powers and had them confirmed by Shaikh Abdul, who gave Abdullah authority to teach the Naqshibandi method. Abdullah worked with many people during the 20 days after the fast, then he and Abdul left for Kabul. On the way they stopped at Ghazni to visit Hakim Sana'i's grave, where Abdullah experienced an ecstatic state. They stayed in Kabul for ten days, working with Shaikh Ibrahim and making arrangements to go to Arabia. To obtain visas from the Arabian Embassy in Kabul it was necessary to swear before a Judge of the High Court of Afghanistan that they were Muslims. In New Zealand this would take about an hour — alas, not so in Afghanistan.

Shaikh Ibrahim sent a man to vouch for the brothers, who telephoned the judge for an appointment. They arrived in reasonable time and the judge sent them to another, who sent them to another, who in turn sent them to another. Each time there was much talking and reading of references, so it was many hours before they were sent back to the second judge, a genial gentleman who did not speak any English. The court was a cell in the basement, about 8' x 16'. People kept coming in and out putting papers on his desk; some of these he would read, then begin haranguing the applicant. He ate snuff and tobacco, constantly using a spittoon alongside his desk, and getting a bull's-eye every time. It was more like Paddy's Market on a Saturday morning than any court, although a great deal of human misery went before their eyes.

Late in the afternoon they were told to come back the next day at 9, and after two hours were given their certificates, which needed to be stamped by the Afghani Foreign Affairs Department and brought back to the High Court. At the Foreign Affairs Department a clerk told them they would have to get a certificate from the British Embassy to say who they were. It was Sunday, and the British Embassy was closed. On Monday the British Embassy signed the certificate and they reported back to the Afghani Court. The judge told them to come back after lunch, and after waiting another hour or so they were given their certificates. Both were amused when the judge told them with a straight face that now they were Muslims, by Koranic law they could be killed if they decided to return to being Christians. He was the first of many to ask them to pray for him when in Mecca.

The certificate was the first step in getting the visas; the next task was to get the actual visa from the Arabian Embassy, so they made arrangements with Shaikh Ibrahim to go at noon the following day. When they arrived at the hotel at 11.30 they were greeted by a man from the Secret Police who made them accompany him under guard to his headquarters, where they were interrogated for an hour and a half then allowed to go. Having missed the appointment at the Arabian Embassy, they decided to go to the police as they had to get an extension for their passports. After a wait of two hours they applied for a five-day extension, which was about to be granted when the head of the department whispered something to the clerk. Next thing they were under guard again, taken under escort to the Shah-I-Nau police station where they were interrogated for three hours, then escorted back to the hotel and told to be out of the country in two days.

Next day they lodged a complaint at the British Embassy about police action both in Kandahar and Kabul, then went to the Arabian Embassy where they were given the best of treatment, getting their visas and letters of recommendation to the Arabian authorities.

There were no bus seats available from Kabul to Peshwar for several days, but on a friend's suggestion they took a mini-bus and next day completed the Customs and police checks at the border without any bother.

Afghanistan appeared to be a police state, and many people told the brothers of friends who had been taken from their homes and shot. Sometimes, when the person was well known, the police classed the death as suicide. This of course is against the teaching of the Holy Prophet, so a double insult was implied. It is Abdullah's considered opinion that within a few years Afghanistan will become a Communist satellite. The ordinary people of over 30 are so ignorant they don't see what is going on. The young people generally are rejecting the Muslim religion, and most of the ones Abdullah spoke to would welcome a change. The majority of the young people ignored the fast of Ramadhan, and from all accounts this also applied in New Zealand. As in all Muslim countries the boys are completely spoiled, so they have inculcated into them the idea of male superiority and selfishness, a combination which produces generally completely unbalanced, egotistical men. The brothers found them always talking down, quoting parrot-fashion from the Koran to prove any point, leaving out any alternative statement which may have contradicted their conditioning. This lack of real intellect on the part of Muslims generally gives them no discernment to enable them to bring the wonderful ideas of the Holy Prophet into the correct perspective. Like the Christian, Buddhist or any other religion, Islam has contained in it great truths and gives a way for its adherents to follow.

What is every religion trying to do for its followers? The main objective must be to lead to a complete understanding of and relationship with God, by whatever name they call Him. The great majority of Muslims are bigots, believing there is no way except theirs, and that the Holy Prophet is the last for all times. If anybody reflects on this assertion they will become aware of the colossal vanity and egotism involved. This goes for most religions; but Abdullah believes, as the Taoist, that though there are many and tortuous ways, they all lead to God.

Their stay in Muslim countries taught the brothers a lot about tolerance, enabling them to see that Allah works through ignorance as well as enlightenment. Friends told of terrible conditions in Afghani jails with up to 40 people in a cell made for six, and no sanitary arrangements whatsoever. The uncle of one friend was so broken after two years in jail, that he died shortly after his release. This friend told them that a week in an Afghani jail, with its indescribable filth and stench of faeces and urine, was equal to a year in any other. The only way to survive was to pay the jailers to get edible food; without this most people did not last many months. This, dear reader, took place during the 1970s, not the 1870s.

Once over the border into Pakistan the brothers proceeded to carry their gear about two furlongs, as the Afghan driver wanted too much to take them to the rail head at Peshwar. Seats for Karachi were all taken for the next few days, but upon learning they were on the Hajj the reservation officer rang Rawalpindi and rearranged some seats to enable them to get on a train leaving that day. It wasn't the fastest train, taking 32 hours to reach Karachi.

They telephoned a contact in Karachi, but received a fairly cool reception, so took a very large room on the third floor of a modestly-priced hotel, which must have been at least 200 years old.

Next day they tried to see a Sufi friend only to find he was away at Lahore, and visited the shipping lines and the Hajj camp to make enquiries about travel to Jeddah. The following day they rang their contact, telling him they had a note from Shaikh Ibrahim, and this time were invited to visit him. Abdullah told Abdul they should do this out of courtesy to Shaikh Ibrahim — it was Abdul who had rung and reported the cool reception. They found Ali to be a very warm and friendly man. It was obvious that he had not been the one who answered the phone to Abdul, as his English was very limited. He modestly explained that he had had very little education and had got where he was by application to work and the grace of Allah. He asked the brothers to be his guests, offering them a flat above one of his factories which they accepted with thanks. Ali arranged for them to go to the Hajj camp to try to get permission to travel to Jeddah by ship, but the Hajj officer advised them to go to the British Consulate, and gave them the name of a man in Islamabad to telephone about getting on a ship.

Their reception by a Mr S. Hinsley at the British Consulate was not in the tradition of English hospitality. The brothers explained they did not speak Urdu, and he commented they weren't there to wet-nurse people. Upon learning that the Hajj people had instructed them to go to the Consulate, he said "They always do this kind of thing," reiterating that the British could not help, as this was asking Christians to get a favour from Muslims. Abdullah thanked him for their appreciation of his loss of blood for England during the war, and said he was sure their Muslim friends would be more helpful than the Christian English. The man had gone noticeably sour when Abdul told him they were Muslims, so his reaction to their request for succour as British citizens in a strange part of the Commonwealth was not surprising. Abdullah's experience as an ordinary traveller has convinced him that English officialdom in the Consulates looks on the hoi polloi as a nuisance whose questions require only the barest civility.

Their Muslim friends made enquiries and found no passage available on a Hajj ship or even one to Bahrain which would get them to Arabia in time, but Ali promised to arrange transport, and eventually they were given free one-way tickets to Medina by Saudi Arabia Airlines.

They decided they would stay for a while in Medina, where the Prophet's tomb is situated, because now they had plenty of time before the Hajj was due to commence. One can visit Mecca at any time to perform Umrah, but Hajj takes place at a set time each year. It moves around the Christian calendar, as the Muslim calendar is based on lunar measurements, and in 1974 was at Christmas time.

Meantime Mian, the Sufi friend, returned and they visited him many times. A great number of people were brought to Abdullah for healing and he became aware that their main negative emotions were worry, fear, insecurity and negative anticipation. Climbing the stairs in a tenement house in the city to see about ten people, he could understand with real compassion why the women had such negative emotions. The appalling conditions would be conducive to all kinds of misery, becoming a hotbed for negativity.

Abdullah believes that about 80 per cent of Muslims who practise their faith do so out of fear of God, living in the pairs of opposites of reward and punishment. He suggested to most of the people he met for healing that they say "Allah give me faith and trust with love", for it is the love of God that is required, not the fear. He explained to them that whenever we put something into action we get a result, which we call either reward or punishment depending on how we see it subjectively. Materialists ask, if God is love why does He let such misery take place? Why should a person be born in such conditions, and why the halt and blind? The answer is that because sufficient people are not available to suffer in a conscious way, many have to suffer in an unconscious way, to provide a certain necessary vibration. The moons, planets, suns and other bodies have to be fed, just like everything on this planet. This has been covered fully in *Probings*, but here it can be said people are born blind or maimed as a result of actions in their past lives. We create our own results, which we call either "reward" or "punishment", by our own "good" or "bad" actions. It is obvious that if God is all-powerful, there can be neither good nor bad, but only God. Relating it to the Law of Three, if an action is done consciously then it is on the active side; if the same action is done unconsciously then it is on the passive side. It is left to the reader to find out the neutralising side. Most Muslims believe in God and the Devil as stated in the Koran. This idea comes from the teaching of Zoroaster, who spoke of Light and Darkness; people don't understand what the third force is. Duality can lead nowhere except into trouble, for, as is said in the Hindu religion, it creates maya or illusion. The fact that so many Muslims approach God out of fear instead of love can be attributed mainly to this idea of God and the Devil.

Arabia and the Hajj

For those readers who know nothing of the Muslim religion it will be helpful to explain what is meant by the Hajj, the discipline the brothers were about to undertake. One of the five pillars of Islam is that every able-bodied Muslim must undertake a pilgrimage to Mecca. It begins when the Hajji leaves his home and prays that he is going to perform, by the grace of Allah, a pilgrimage to Mecca. There are set prayers, coming from the time of Mohammed, for every step of the way, even a prayer for mounting a camel or horse.

When approaching Mecca from North, South, East or West, there are definite boundaries where the Hajji puts on his Ehram robes, which consist of two unhemmed sheets 7' x 4'6", one worn around the waist to the ankles, the other over the shoulders. No hat is worn by the men, the women have their faces uncovered and wear usual dress. The idea behind the Ehram robes is that all men, whatever their station in life, look the same in the sight of God. Once the robes are put on then people must observe several taboos. There is to be no sex play, intercourse, or talk, no fighting, hunting, putting on of perfume, clipping or shaving of hair, or covering of the head by a man. No sewn clothing can be worn by the man; one must be careful when scratching the head that no lice or hair fall.

It is Sunnat (good) to have a bath before entering Mecca with the right foot first and saying the appropriate prayer. At the Ka'aba there is a prayer for each circuit of the stone. In the crush of the Hajj a person will have great difficulty carrying out such things as kissing the Hayar-i-Aswad or caressing Rukn-i-Yamaanee. Elsewhere it is Makrooh (wrong) to kiss or touch any other wall of the Ka'aba. It is wrong to eat, buy, or sell whilst doing the seven circuits of the Ka'aba. After, one does two Ra'akats of Tawaaf, goes to the well of Zam Zam and has a drink of water, then returns to Hayar-i-Aswad, embraces it and prays again. Next one performs Sa'ee, running between the two hillocks, Safa and Marwah.

All pilgrims have to go to Mina, three miles from Mecca, after the sun has risen; it is expected that one spend the night there. The following morning at daybreak the pilgrims should go to Arafaat where they join in communal prayers following an Imam (prayer leader). After this the pilgrim goes on to Wakoof-i-Muzdalafah, to stand from mid-day to sunset praying constantly, with raised hands. The hands and arms are not held aloft continuously, but for the time it takes to say two Ra'akats; that is to say, about three minutes rest and three minutes of raised hands. After sunset the pilgrim departs for Muzdalafah, three miles away, where one should remain awake all night, praying. In the morning the pilgrim goes to Mina, in the vicinity of which four rites take place, called Ramee, Nahr, Halq, and Tawaaf-i-Ziyaarat. Ramee is the pelting of seven pebbles picked up at Muzdalafah, repeated seven times in different places. Usually, however, this is done only three times. Nahr is the sacrifice of an animal; Halq is the shaving of the head of men; Tawaaf-i-Ziyaarat is going around the Ka'aba seven times.

It is also encumbent on the pilgrim to pay homage to the Prophet's tomb at Medina about four hundred miles from Mecca; again there are prayers laid down for this.

To the non-Muslim the Hajj would appear strange, to say the least, but it has its esoteric significance which unfortunately is not understood by most of the pilgrims.

The Hajj was initiated in the time of the Prophet

Abraham, who was born approximately 2000 B.C., and who preached the worship of one God. When his enemies made things hard for him he and his wife Sarah went to Egypt, where the Pharaoh was kind to him, giving him his daughter Hagar when Abraham returned to his own country.

Abraham was childless up to an old age and, according to history, prayed for a child and had his wish granted; first Hagar had Ismail, then Sarah had Isaac. The two sons created a problem so Abraham was advised by God to take Hagar and Ismail to the place in the desert where the Ka'aba now stands, where he was to leave them with a few dates and a water skin. As he left Hagar she asked him whether he was rejecting her or following God's command. He told her he was following God's instructions, so she was satisfied and acquiesced. He prayed to God to protect Hagar and Ismail, because it was a very desolate place.

After a while the dates and water were used up and the two became very thirsty. This made the baby Ismail cry, Hagar became worried, and desperately ran between the hillocks, Safa and Marwah, but could not locate water. She did this seven times, and each time when she got to the top of the hills she prayed to God for succour. Her prayers were answered because under the place the baby rubbed his heels, came bubbling the waters of Zam Zam. She hurriedly built up the earth around the water, and the Holy Prophet used to say that had she not done this the waters would have flooded the earth. Hagar and Ismail stayed in solitude for five days, then were joined by a tribe of desert people, and thus commenced the city of Mecca.

Much later Abraham came to visit Hagar, as he had seen in a dream that he was to sacrifice his son, Ismail. When Ismail was old enough Abraham recounted the dream, and Ismail told his father to carry out the divine command. As the father and son were going to do the sacrifice, Satan tried to dissuade them from the task. Abraham threw seven pebbles in three places and each time Satan turned into a stone. When Abraham was about to kill his son he found that God was only testing his faith — an angel took Ismail away, substituting a ram in his place.

Ismail grew up and married a girl of the Jurhum tribe which had settled near Zam Zam and befriended Hagar and the child. When Abraham turned up for the third time and asked Ismail for help to re-build the Ka'aba he was delighted to be of assistance to his father. Ismail carried the stones and Abraham laid them in place. When the job was completed God then commanded Abraham to give the call to the world for people to come on the Hajj. After the call Abraham and his good son went around the Ka'aba seven times.

The building was once repaired by the Jurhum tribe, once by an Amalakite king of Egypt and Syria, and the third time by the Qurish tribe at the time of the Prophet, but a little before he received the call. It was at this time that the Holy Prophet showed indications of his future sagacity. The tribesmen were going to commence fighting one another for the privilege of replacing the black stone, when the Holy Prophet suggested that they put him and the stone on a big mat; the tribesmen standing all around lifted the load simultaneously, and the Prophet put the stone into a niche in the wall. The Ka'aba has been rebuilt several times since.

The reader will immediately see the Laws of Three and Seven in this story, and realise that the Hajj is the playing out of Hagar's fate. The story of the sacrifice shows on the surface how man is repaid by faith, but under this is the esoteric truth that one cannot hold onto youth. The ram as a symbol of sexual virility indicates the conquest of lust. Many Muslims believe that the Hajj is symbolic of the lover and his Beloved, the Hajji being intoxicated by the love of God, going hither and thither in search of the goal. There are many explanations of the Hajj by Muslim theologians, most of which follow a very literal line, as is customary in the Muslim world. Anything in the Hadith or Koran is held to be true, no matter how far-fetched to objective reasoning. The Koran, like the Bible, has inaccuracies caused by the ego of writers intruding into the universal truths.

An uneventful flight from Karachi landed the brothers in Medina at about 10.30 p.m. Saudi Arabian time as adjusted to G.M.T. The Arabians also have a system of time which starts from sunset, or Maghrib prayers, instead of midnight as in European time.

Customs inspection took about an hour. Officials went through all Abdullah's luggage and confiscated a book of Ramdas, saying it was "against their religion". He asked if they could hold it until he left the country, but they were unco-operative. He was sorry to part with this book, inscribed with Ramnam in Sanskrit by Mother Krishnabai, which he had carried for a number of years and read whenever he had spare time. This action on the part of the customs was typical of the bigotry of many Muslims, who observe only the outside part of the religion.

A fellow-passenger on the plane had advised the brothers to stay at a Masjid El Noor, because accommodation would be difficult to find at that hour of night. Abdullah was agreeable to this, because of promptings from within, but Abdul spoke to one of the customs men and arranged for them to go elsewhere. They arrived at a broken-down ruin and after a half-hour wait were shown to the third floor of an adjacent building. The bare room, with dirt all around the edges and cracked walls, was about 8' x 12'. A sort of cupboard had a hole in the concrete used as a toilet, with a tap nearby. The only decoration was a Honda calendar, with the model's head cut out and something written in Arabic. Two squabs were brought for beds on the concrete floor, so they pulled out their sleeping bags and bunked down for the night.

In the morning Abdullah suggested that Abdul go to the University with a letter from Mian, their Sufi friend, addressed to an old friend of his asking him to help find accommodation. After about three hours

Abdul came back and reported he would need a lot longer to find Mian's friend, but that he had contacted a Hajj agent with whom their luggage could be left, allowing them to get out of the room they were in. The door on this room had no lock and there was an opening from another passage, so Abdullah agreed. When they went to pay for the room they were asked for 700 Rial, which was about $US180. Abdullah laughed and offered 6 Rial. The proprietors came down to 400 Rial, which was stupid, so Abdullah told them to come with them to the agent. After a lot of noise they came down to 15 Rial, which Abdullah said was still stupid, maintaining his offer of 6 Rial. They went away, and that was the last the brothers heard of them.

While Abdullah stayed with the luggage, Abdul went to change some money then return to the University. After about two hours he arrived back with two men, and the news that Mian's friend was now head of the Tablig group at the Masjid El Noor. Abdullah smiled, knowing full well this had been intended right from the beginning and all the previous carrying on had been to teach them a thing or two. The four set off for the Masjid, leaving the luggage with the agent. They walked over a mile, through a tin shanty town inhabited by erstwhile slaves, then the local rubbish tip which stank to high heaven. The alleys were thronged with goats and kids, dirty children, and adult beggars. Half-inch plastic hoses ran from taps in the streets into mud brick houses. Everywhere, flies and shit, both human and animal. It was typical of the conditions many people in the East have to live under.

The brothers settled into a room at the Masjid El Noor, which means Church of Light. There were the usual squabs on the hard floor, with five recesses in the block walls containing plenty of other people's bits and pieces. The room was 12' x 10' and most nights slept six, sometimes seven. The people who ran this mosque were part of the Tablig school, traditionalists trying to keep the clock back in the days of the Holy Prophet, who would slavishly follow many of the injunctions given in the Hadith or traditions of the Prophet.

Muslims maintain there are no monks in Islam, but this type of situation belied the assertion. The brothers lived the life of a monk at Masjid El Noor, getting up at 4.30 for prayers, doing their ablutions at a cold tap which often was the merest trickle and on a few occasions not even that so they would have to store water to use out of one of the spouted pots. Prayers were going on constantly as well as the five communal prayers. In between, someone was always lecturing others. There was a continual stream of visitors from among the pilgrims, for the Tablig school are the missionaries of Islam. They call themselves the Jumat (brothers) and go to other mosques to waylay people and harangue them constantly, trying to influence them back to their religion. They also attempt to convert any infidel they find interested in Islam. They are all most sincere, trying to live to the Koran, and most are very fearful and superstitious. Some are bigoted although most were found to be friendly, and definitely acting as brothers. Abdullah and Abdul were able to respond and went out of their way to understand their motives and conditioning.

The Holy Prophet's ideas on cleanliness were a thousand years ahead of his time, for when the people of Europe were having a bath only once a year, if at all, the Prophet had his people bathing once a week. However, the Law of Seven has caught up with this, and now the Muslim people must contend for first place among the dirtiest races in the world. At El Noor there was never any hot water for a bath, and most people used no soap; this applied for wuzu, the ceremonial washing of hands and feet before prayers. Often there was no water at all because the town was so overcrowded the system could not cope. There were no flush toilets, but pans let into the floors with an adjacent tap, and even when there was water about half the users would not wash away their stool. To add to the lack of hygiene, the cookhouse was adjacent to the toilets.

Most of the people there were very pleasant and friendly. Many came to talk to Abdullah, some to learn, others to teach him the right way as they saw it through the Koran and Hadith. He formed the opinion that most were identified with sex and devil, for these usually came into the conversation. As has been said elsewhere, Muslims are obsessed with reward and punishment, and much of their attitude toward sex is very archaic. The penalty for adultery is stoning to death, and in recent years a Christian at Jeddah killed a Muslim he caught in bed with his wife, so the Muslim's friends and relatives killed the Christian by running over him with a truck. Most who spoke to Abdullah had not the slightest idea of sex psychology, still believing women to be the instrument of the devil. One young South African Indian who came each night for a chat summed up this primitive conception of sex when he observed that "women are the trouble". Much latent homosexual behaviour noticed among Muslim friends stemmed from sexual frustrations. The South African Indian friend told Abdullah with a very straight face that the devil was in the toilet and you should always cough before going in left foot first, being careful to wear your hat. Whoever told him about the devil must have been referring to masturbation — it wasn't clear why he had to keep his hat on.

The Emir wouldn't let Abdullah smoke his pipe in the room, although the Jumat brothers ate betel nut and spat copiously. Smoking is not condemned in Islam but frowned upon by many of the more orthodox Muslims who inevitably chew betel nut or take snuff — which often contains tobacco — with the attending coughing, spitting, and sneezing. When Abdullah wanted a smoke he would go for a walk around the back alleys, and this way saw a bit of village life. Abdullah smoked mainly as a compensation to the body, which was obedient and deserved some relaxation. He never smoked when fasting, and found it no trouble to go without at any time.

The only two Europeans at El Noor were attending the Medina University. One was a Dutchman, married to an Egyptian, the other a Dane whose wife was still in Denmark. Both were quite fanatical about the Prophet and Hadith, although the Dutchman was not quite sure if he had found the truth. Abdullah tried to get him to give his own conception of Allah but he had to draw on the Koran. Another interesting man, a former Olympic representative for his country, was very unsure of himself, and after some time Abdullah became aware that he was confused between the literal and esoteric teaching of the Koran. He had ended up with recurring migraine headaches, so Abdullah gave him a mantram: "Allah deliver me from insecurity, fear, anger, and give me love".

One Arabian member of the Jumat, who was interested in Abdullah because he heard he was a Sufi, came to him with many questions, and although he was narrow in his following of the literal commands of the Koran and Hadith and had patterned his life on the daily external actions of the Prophet, wanted to know why Abdullah did not worry about praying, prostrating or the strict observance of wuzu before prayers. He was after the reward of becoming a Man No. 4, although he did not understand the whole method. From within Abdullah was told to teach him, so he did, asking him to keep the knowledge to himself, as the orthodox brothers would certainly be upset at some of the truth he was expounding. The permanent brother in the room, a Kenyan Indian who had been living at El Noor for more than a year, heard a bit of the conversation and became very antagonistic towards Abdullah, so he had to close up when this man was around. Before Abdullah left, he told his Arabian friend the story of Chick Pea being put in the Holy of Holies for the night, with the hope that the Arabian would be able to piss on his own false idols. Having lived for 16 days with these brothers, Abdullah had become more aware just how hard it was for anyone to wake up to the inaccuracies of the exoteric teachings of Islam. The brainwashing was, and is, very constant. Abdullah remembered that when Neil was about 17 he read the *Martyrdom of Man*, by Winwood Reade, and because of his ignorance rejected the exoteric Christian religion completely, without any understanding of the esoteric teaching. Many people, like Joseph McCabe, wrote books refuting Christianity because they made similar mistakes. Neil decided he would not pray again, and when he missed his first prayers half felt that the roof would fall in, then as the days passed became more sure of himself so that for many years he didn't pray, even when in great danger as a soldier.

At this time of year, Medina, a typical Muslim town with streets of bazaars, derelict buildings, mud-brick houses, hotels and mosques, was crowded with pilgrims. The Haram Sharief, which housed the Prophet's tomb, was a beautiful building with two pairs of minarets, built at different times. The very old Mausoleum dome had been renovated by the Turks when they occupied the Arabian Empire well before the First World War. The mosque covered about two acres and adjacent was a seven-acre open court being temporarily covered with pre-cast fibreglass domes, where a new wing was to be built.

When a pilgrim visits the tomb of the Prophet there are set prayers to be said and it is also expected that one perform forty communal prayers at the mosque without a break. At five prayers a day, one has to stay at least eight days. The place was full when Abdullah and Abdul started the forty communal prayers, and after a week the crowd was so impossible that to get a place in the mosque one had to be prepared to wait for two to three hours before the call. The large court filled up and the roads adjacent to the mosque were packed. The crowd was very boisterous, jostling and shoving to get a place. This zeal was attributable to the fact that the majority of pilgrims were concerned with the reward of worshipping at this tomb, believing that one

Ra'akat said in the Haram Sharief was equal to seventy thousand said elsewhere. You could almost see them counting up their credits. The brothers decided to get close to the Prophet's tomb for one prayer, so arrived more than three hours before the service; when they started to pray people were still fighting for a place. Directly in front of them one man was lifted bodily by two others from where he was standing. When praying as a Muslim there should be a space of about three feet between the rows, but many ignorant people like this man would sit where you were about to put your head, then, when you stood up to commence the prayers, try to push into the rows without any thought or concern that you had been waiting much longer than he. Abdullah was amazed at the number of women pilgrims, the majority of whom were quite old; indeed there were very few women under 50 years. In the street they pushed and shoved with the best, hanging on to each others' robes, proceeding like a row of ducks, and woe betide you if you got in their way — they were quite capable of pushing you over. The men would complain bitterly if women got in between them and Mecca while praying, so in the mosque they were always at the back. In the streets there were many wrangles as the women pushed in anywhere. Men would leave a space rather than pray directly behind women, and as it did not trouble the brothers they would take up these places.

The mosque had a good atmosphere despite these goings-on, and great beauty, both inside and out. It was unfortunate for the reasonable pilgrim that the authorities didn't have a better system, such as making people go in one direction about the mosque and leaving passageways to walk. The traders who peddled everything from beads to carpets tended to become tiresome, walking with their dirty feet over the prayer-mat where you were about to put your head. Abdullah was reminded of the story in the Christian Bible of Christ throwing the traders out of the temple. It was a real test of one's endurance and concentration to perform anything other than the set prayers, which were controlled by the Imam via a loudspeaker and done simultaneously by the entire congregation. The brothers wanted to, and did, many extra prayers under fairly difficult conditions which Abdullah believed were there to teach something.

On one particular day at the Haram Sharief, Abdullah was told from within to pray on the right side of the Prophet's tomb, looking towards Mecca, as this was where the best vibrations were centred. He did this for a few days, until he was given Universal Vision; then he was told he could go anywhere. It was becoming increasingly difficult to get through the crowds. After the Universal Vision he prayed in the street adjacent to the mosque, or in the plaza.

When the brothers had completed their forty consecutive prayers they prayed mainly at the El Noor mosque, as the crowds around the Haram Sharief were impossible.

One day there was very heavy rain, the heaviest in years according to the locals, and the next day more than half the crowd had colds which were to persist for the rest of the brothers' stay.

Muslims do not believe in idols, and wherever they have conquered have destroyed priceless works of art by breaking off the faces; but unfortunately they have made idols of their shrines, with people fighting to touch a sacred place. A great deal of the pushing and shoving at Haram Sharief is attributable to this idolisation. Objectively watching people around the Prophet's grave, one could only come to the conclusion that they have created an idol here. Nearby are some of the Prophet's wives' graves, and the crying and touching of the walls is no different from what goes on in Catholic countries.

In Saudi Arabia, the classic Muslim law prescribes the cutting off of the right hand as the penalty for stealing, but Abdul had his new white gown cut at the pocket and the money he was carrying taken. Other people told of similar experiences. During the Hajj season the prices for everything were exorbitant, as the shopkeepers had no conscience about profiteering. The brothers could speak next to no Arabic so were at a disadvantage in doing any bargaining, but many pilgrims who had some knowledge of the language engaged in great quarrelling about charges, apparently very shocked at what they had to pay for food.

The brothers cooked their own food, as their stomachs were rather sensitive compared to the native population. They didn't buy meat, as it was always covered in flies and cost over a dollar a pound for stewing quality. They bought bread as it came out of the ovens, covering it up from the flies immediately, made vegetable soup, and ate porridge, boiled eggs, concoctions with tinned fish, and any fruit they could get. They found such things as dried fruit couldn't be eaten raw, so cooked these too. Yoghurt was readily available everywhere and had no ill effects. The ordinary pilgrims from Muslim countries seemed to have their share of stomach troubles, as the brothers noted a lot of pills being taken.

On 15 December Abdullah and Abdul left with one of the brothers from El Noor for Mecca, taking a taxi to a railway station which had not been used as such since the lines had been blown up by Lawrence in 1916. The yards adjacent were used as a bus and taxi depot for travellers leaving Medina. After an hour they settled on a taxi to Mecca shared between five people at double the usual price, as the taxi drivers were opportunists, making hay while the Hajj sun was shining. At the first road block the police would not let them past, as the law had been changed two days before, making it compulsory for people to leave Medina by the same form of transport as they arrived — in the brothers' case by plane. As they had special diplomatic passes from the Arabian Embassy in Afghanistan, entitling them to go by road if they wanted, they were determined to follow this course. However, in spite of what the Arabian Embassy had told them the police turned them back. At the bus depot the irate driver threw their luggage out on the ground and then wanted extra Rials for his trouble. Abdullah refused to pay, as the driver was getting double the ordinary fare from his new passengers. The Jumat brother who accompanied them from El Noor was a very slender reed who left them to their discomforts — a pity, because he could have interpreted for them. It was decided that Abdul should go to the El Noor mosque and get someone who spoke English to help him obtain the required permission to go by road, while Abdullah stayed to mind the luggage as it was in open ground and there was nowhere available to store it. After six hours Abdul arrived back with two brothers, one of whom spoke Arabic and Urdu, the other Urdu and English. They had got the stamp of officialdom after a very trying time for Abdul, who with Abdullah was fasting for three days on only water and was beginning to feel the strain. Before they were able to negotiate with a new taxi, the Jumat brothers decided they must go to the nearest mosque to say their Ishar prayers, so there was another hour's wait. Finally the haggling with the taxi driver was completed and they started off again, stopping just before the road block to enable one of the other passengers to perform his wuzu and change into his Ehram clothes. It was also necessary for the group to say two Ra'akats, making known to Allah their intention and humbly asking His acceptance of their efforts to perform Umrah, or the lesser pilgrimage. Having passed the first road block successfully the brothers were able to relax while two other passengers said prayers aloud, the driver and another talked incessantly, and for good measure the radio blared at top volume. After an hour there was the first of three stops for tea, but as they were fasting the brothers didn't get a drink. After five hours' travelling they were dropped off at 1 a.m., at a building they were told was their destination. However, on waking up a figure at the window they were informed by pointing and gesturing while chanting the name Al Fihr, that Masjid Al Fihr was a few hundred yards away. They had already carried their gear a fair way from where the taxi had set them down, so rather than go off on a wild goose chase decided to go and investigate.

They found a mosque and hammered on the door, but there was no reply. Just as they were returning to their gear a man walked past who, on being questioned, showed an open door and indicated a mosque which was down the drive. This man arrived back at the first mosque as they were loading up and very kindly carried Abdul's large pack on top of his head, enabling them to do the transference in one trip. They dumped everything in the mosque among a hundred or so sleeping bodies, then going outside, proceeded to follow other pilgrims up the hill. It was now nearly 2 a.m., but there were many people walking and cars tooting their way up the long hill. At the top, the minarets of the Haram Sharief were visible in the distance down the other side of the hill, so following their noses they eventually arrived at one of the large doors leading into the mosque.

The name Haram Sharief was used both for the Prophet's tomb in Medina and this mosque which contained the Ka'aba in Mecca. (Haram means "sacred precinct".) The building, which Egyptian engineers had finished only recently at a cost of 50 million Rial, could house a million people. Seven minarets, not five as the prayer mats show, had tops made of pure gold. The architecture, with all the hundreds of domes laced together, reminded Abdullah a little of St. Peter's in Rome.

The brothers entered and proceeded down the marble steps, then both drew their breaths as they saw, standing in the middle of an open space, the Ka'aba in all its austerity. It was a large cube-shaped building draped in black curtains covered with Arabic inscriptions and at this early hour hundreds of pilgrims were performing their Tawaaf, seven circuits of the Ka'aba. Joining in, the brothers were carried along with the crowds which pushed and jostled in the usual manner.

Each pilgrim should have the chance of kissing the black stone (most likely a meteorite), but it was impossible to get near the walls of the Ka'aba because of the fighting for places. Abdullah had no intention of competing in this hurly-burly, so just drifted around the outside of the cauldron trying to absorb what vibrations he could. At the end of the seven circuits he became aware that the fighting had negated any good vibrations which should have been available outside the immediate area of the Ka'aba, so that the main vibrational field would be inside the actual building while this type of behaviour went on.

At 3 a.m. they decided to go back to the Al Fihr mosque to get an hour's rest before Fajar prayers at 5.30. They rolled out their sleeping bags on the marble floor of the mosque but stayed awake till they were called at 4.30 to go back to the Haram Sharief. They told the Emir they would pray at the Al Fihr, and were shown where to put their gear in a room with six others. Later there were several more in this room, so the brothers decided to sleep on the roof of the mosque. Abdullah stayed one night in the room, to be sociable, but had a very uncomfortable time with the heat and stench of bodies, for these people liked the door closed and no appreciable amount of air came through the screen windows, one of which was shut. Two negroes, a South African Indian and Abdullah went to bed at 9.30, an hour later two South African negroes came in, putting the lights on, and there were two further arrivals. Eventually, at about 1, everything was quiet, then at 4.30 they were awakened by the call of the Emir, "Haram Sharief, Haram Sharief!" The latecomers were still sleeping when the call "Azan" was performed at 5.30.

The brothers were told they should complete Umrah by doing the seven passages between the hills of Safa and Marwah, and visiting the Zam Zam springs. A very pleasant Egyptian in the next room said he would take them and recite the prayers. So off they went to the Haram Sharief dressed as pilgrims again. The

Egyptian took them in the correct gate to perform the Sa'ee, the re-enactment of the movements of Hagar running between the two hills to find water for her son, Ismail. There was now a long marble building with the two hills showing only their tops in the rough volcanic stone, the rest being paved with marble slabs. Down the middle were two carriageways for wheelchairs.

The pilgrims started from the hill called Safa, and walked down the passage, about 30 feet wide by a thousand yards long, which ran each side of the wheelchair ways. At one point there was a green mark, where you were expected to run each time until you got to the next green mark. These were called Meelain-i-Aghdarain, or the two green miles. After passing the second green mark you resumed walking. The first slopes of each hill were covered in grooved tiles, the crown was the rough rock. At each hill, you turned and faced the Ka'aba, crying out "Allah O Akbar" three times. After finishing the seven walks at Marwah, men pilgrims were expected to have their hair cut, although it was more correct to have the head shaved.

Zam Zam was in the same area as the Haram Sharief. The brothers struggled down the steps which led to the well, but when they eventually did get near the water there was a real fight going on among the pilgrims, so Abdullah decided he had had enough and struggled back up the steps again. Later a friendly Turk offered him a drink of Zam Zam water which he accepted, drinking half and pouring the rest over his head, as he had had his hair cut short and the sun was pelting down remorselessly on his bald pate.

The crowds were daily becoming larger so the brothers found it was more convenient to pray at the Al Fihr mosque than to struggle up the hills being manhandled by the huge unruly throngs. However, they made a visit to the Haram Sharief each day for at least one communal prayer. The people at the Al Fihr mosque were the same types as at El Noor, containing both good and bad qualities. Abdul got his fair measure of lectures by well-intending bigots, and even

Abdullah did not escape completely. The brothers attended some of the talks, finding the system was the same, with people expounding but no discussion afterwards, only someone else reiterating what had been said before. When they tried to open a discussion they were cut off and given a further lecture. Everything was taken literally from the Koran and the Hadith with no one trying to see the esoteric side, so after a while they gave up and remained silent.

A fellow who had been living in Australia for two years approached Abdullah and spoke of his search for knowledge of the Sufis. He had been told by a Pakistani doctor in Australia to go to an address in Karachi, but found his contact to be unsatisfactory so had come to Arabia, where he was only allowed to stay three days. After that he had to go to his homeland, Egypt, to get a visa to return to Saudi Arabia. He said he had not been able to practise his religion properly in Australia as most of the Muslims were not very thorough in their religious practices, so had turned to reading. When he came across Al Ghazali he was impressed, and decided to pursue the Sufi line of thought while keeping within the Muslim fold. He spoke to Abdullah over several days, asking very good questions, appearing to be courageous enough to cope with the task ahead of him. Abdullah's main advice to him was to become a good householder — to marry, practise his religion sincerely from within by being in the world, but not of the world; also to learn discernment between the inner and outer teaching of Islam.

On the Friday before the Hajj started, the brothers went to the Haram Sharief with over a million others to do the mid-day prayers, or Jumuh. They saw armed guards tossing people off the main entrance to the mosque to make room for VIPs who arrived hours later than the waiting pilgrims. Abdullah couldn't get into the mosque proper, but remained in the street with thousands of others. The conditions outside were chaotic. Nearby was a truck with a machinegun mounted on its back directed towards the main door, and Abdullah wondered what would happen to the congregation if the gunner had to fire it. These precautions were taken to give protection to King Faisal and his ministers.

The Hajj started after early morning prayers on Sunday 22nd December. Abdullah and Abdul were ready to go with the Jumat brothers at 6 but after the usual wait eventually started walking to Mina at 7.30. Mina is about five miles from Mecca, and as the Prophet was accustomed to walk, it is considered the correct thing to do. It was very hot, they were carrying bedding and other camping gear, so didn't arrive till about 11. Thousands of people on the road plus all kinds of vehicles tended to make progress very slow. They chanted continually in Arabic "Labbaika Allahamma Labbaka Rabbaika Leashareeka Laka Labbaik" as they wended their way in and out of the traffic. These words were an invocation to God or Allah, signifying that you were here and offering your Hajj to Him. The brothers' Egyptian friend, Moosa, was the life of the party, running up and down the straggling line, chanting like a cheer-leader at a football match.

Abdullah and Abdul were attached to the Egyptians; when they reached Mina Moosa left Abdullah with the baggage and, accompanied by Abdul, went to find his friends who had gone by truck. They came back a short while later and escorted Abdullah to the Egyptian brothers who were friendly with one of the policemen and had made a rough shelter alongside a police tent. Abdul and Abdullah were allotted about three feet, and proceeded to use an Ehram sheet for a cover from the blazing sun. They were close to the main mosque at the corner of the street which was crowded with pilgrims and parked vehicles. The hospital was opposite so they were kept awake by the noise of the busy ambulances as they blasted on the sirens to try to get through the crowds. Many people died, and at one time the Egyptians counted ten dead stacked in an ambulance. Conditions were archaic, with very little water and only one hundred public

toilets for one and a half million people. A great deal of
the time these toilets were closed through lack of
water, and under guard. The streets became a
quagmire of excreta and urine, especially behind the
parked vehicles.

The object of going to Mina was to do five consecutive prayers in the same way as the Holy Prophet
did, four on the day of arrival and the fifth the next
morning before dawn, thus all had to sleep the night in
Mina. There were few hotels and the majority of
pilgrims hired tents from their guides, so there were
thousands of tents spread over the countryside. A
great number of people slept in the streets, as the
brothers did, or in the mosque if they could find a place
to doss down. It was very mountainous behind the
mosque but every available position was taken by the
pilgrims. Abdullah and Abdul were both used to camping so were able to adapt easily enough to the conditions, cooking their meals on a small benzene stove.

After a very fitful night's sleep the brothers completed the Fajar prayers at Mina and hired a small
truck to go to Arafat. They stopped at a very large
mosque called Masjid-I- Namdaram, unloaded their
gear, then took up positions inside for three and a half
hours until mid-day prayers. As time passed the place
became more crowded, till the usual situation prevail-
ed, with people pushing and wrestling each other,
climbing over seated people, some struggling one way
and others in the opposite direction. All the
passageways soon became occupied, causing complete
chaos, with real fights going on all over the place.

As the hour of prayer drew near, people appeared to
become quite mad in their endeavours to gain a place in
which to pray. The brothers made room for two old
Turks by squeezing together, but this didn't stop two
others pushing in, thus making it almost impossible
for the Turks to find a place to put their heads in
prayer. The hysteria of these people had to be seen to
be believed. Abdullah observed to Abdul that one
could easily see the mis-use of sex energy in all these ir-

rational actions. The Saudi Government had no organisation to cope with this vast horde of people, so there was no crowd control in the mosques at all, unless they wanted to make way for some personage. The whole Saudi nation appeared to be concerned only with making money from the pilgrims, whom they exploited to the fullest limits. Every commodity was at least double the usual price, according to the friends who lived in Medina.

After this mad service the brothers had lunch in the mosque then proceeded to carry their gear along the road to Arafat. In about half an hour the Egyptians said they had arrived, as they were in the region of Arafat; although the mountain was a mile away it was permissible to stop where they were until sunset. The mountain was much smaller than Abdullah had imagined and appeared to be crowded with people, so he was happy to stay where they were, knowing by previous experiences what would be going on up the mountain. The Egyptians said that each year someone was pushed down and killed in the scramble. With the gear alongside some buses, they waited for sunset. From all accounts, Prophet Abraham used to pray at Arafat, and the Holy Prophet did the same. From midday until sunset he used to stand with his hands raised above his head for approximately three minutes, then would have three minutes' rest, and so on. At sunset they trudged a mile to another road, as the one they were on was completely jammed for miles, and after a couple of hours' wait secured a truck to Muzdalafah, where they spent the night among the rocks. The Holy Prophet also stayed here, praying all the night; now people said prayers in groups then went to sleep on the ground.

In the morning after dawn prayers, everybody picked up pebbles in preparation for the pelting of the idols at Mina. Returning on foot, they found their places by the police tent had been taken, but this didn't deter the Egyptians who muscled in and made a heap of their gear. Half the group were sent away to pelt the first idol, while the others watched their possessions. It is said the devil tempted Abraham three times, and each time he retaliated by throwing seven pebbles at him, turning him into a rock; thus the Holy Prophet instructed his followers to emulate his example. Abdullah went with the first group, Abdul with the second. It was impossible to get near the idol unless you were unconcerned about being hit by the flying pebbles, and there was such a crush within a hundred feet of the idol that you couldn't get your hands above your head. Before attacking this situation, the Egyptians tied their Ehram sheets tightly around their money and possessions, because they knew that thieves operated in the vicinity of this idol, taking advantage of the fact that if a person had his hands above his head there was no way of checking on purses. Abdullah made a token job of the pelting and returned to the rendezvous. When it was Abdul's turn he was pushed over by a group of negroes who charged him down, and lost his watch. The behaviour was completely stupid, again with no direction from the authorities, who could easily have controlled the flow of people.

By now Abdul and Abdullah were completely disgusted with this type of conduct so decided to leave Mina, although most people stay there for three days to throw the pebbles and also sacrifice an animal, which both found repugnant for several reasons. They clipped their hair, another ritual performed on this first day at Mina after Arafat, then told the Egyptians they were going back to Mecca and would return the next day to throw more pebbles at the other idols, to comply with the conditions of the Hajj.

The mosque at Mecca where they were staying was locked, so Abdul climbed the fence and let Abdullah in. They slept on the roof in comparative peace after doing Tawaaf, the seven circuits around the Ka'aba which is the fourth task after Arafat. Here again the crowd behaved ridiculously, with absolutely no control. Abdullah was one of many who had their shoes stolen.

Next day they went along the top road, about eight

hundred feet above Mina, in an endeavour to miss some of the crowd. The whole street where the vehicles were parked was one great cesspool with filth everywhere; when they came down the mountainside they found pieces of animal along with the excreta and tents. The Egyptians were cutting up a leg of camel, which seven of them had shared in the sacrifice, and had some ram and goat meat as well. The camel had cost them 1000 Rial ($US300). They gave the brothers some, which they took back to Mina and made into soup. One of the Egyptians was a veterinarian who used to laugh at their cooking, saying that Egyptians had stronger stomachs. However, they all had dysentery the next day, while the brothers were both fit, no doubt because they washed and cleaned the meat before cooking, whereas the Egyptians appeared to be very careless with their preparations.

They wanted Abdullah to go to the main sacrificial area to see what was going on, but he knew the waste must be substantial and didn't want to look at it, as the peasant in him hated such disrespect to our Holy Mother the Earth. Abdul went, and his impressions of this spectacle are recorded elsewhere in this book. He was disgusted at this ultimate stupidity, with dead animals three deep all over the area and bulldozers burying them in trenches. Blood-bespeckled people killed more while others encouraged them, looking on with glazed eyes at the carnage. This was about the way Abdullah had predicted it would be, before Abdul went.

They didn't return to Mina for the third pelting of the idols the following day, because they felt it would be almost impossible to get close enough to the idols to be effective. Also, they'd decided they had paid enough attention to the Law of Seven.

A few days later, at Jeddah, Abdullah boarded a plane for Karachi and Abdul left by road for Jordan on his way to Europe. Thus they completed the Hajj, and became entitled to the prefix Hajji in front of their names.

It is a great pity for the sincere pilgrims that the Saudi Government does not control the crowds better, to enable them more orderly access to these sacred places. This year, speaking only from what Abdullah observed, most of the spritual character of the Hajj was lost to sheer survival. The ignorance of many pilgrims is abysmal, thus putting so many people together is fraught with great hazards. The lack of organisation, and rapacity of the shopkeepers, taxi-drivers, hotel keepers, etc., must be laid at the door of King Faisal and his Government. It is for them to rectify the situation by tighter crowd control along with stringent price control, otherwise they will reap their reward. There must be more toilets, with plenty of water, to avert sickness amongst the pilgrims, half of whom, by the evidence on the streets, were suffering from dysentery.

Abdullah does not regret going on the Hajj, as it taught him a great deal about Muslims and about himself, but he would certainly warn the weak in health to be careful in undertaking this task.

The impressions of
Abdul and Zaid

Some months before leaving New Zealand, Neil and Abdullah had found from within that to give an objective account of the impending fast it would be desirable to have impressions from three types of men. This led Neil to invite two of his pupils to accompany him on the trip, Chris, or Abdul Rahman, an intellectual man, and Denis, or Zaid, an emotional man. Neil was a moving-instinctive man originally, although he was balanced in his three centres when the journey began.

Here it may be appropriate to explain the use of the Muslim names. Gurdjieff always called people "such and such an idiot", or "rabbit", "mouse", etc. while Hazrat Inayat Khan gave Muslim names. Abdullah preferred Muslim names because he saw in Gurdjieff a certain quality of negativeness — the labels he gave to people were what they happened to be when Gurdjieff worked with them, whereas Muslim names gave people an aim to work for to raise themselves above the state they were in when they met Neil and Abdullah. This negative quality of Gurdjieff's could be seen in many of his teachings, such as his saying that the only hope for mankind was for people to see, when they looked at each other, that each had to die. Neil and Abdullah preferred to think that each has to live. Gurdjieff and Abdullah are equally right of course.

Abdul and Zaid demonstrate their respective types by their questions during the fast, and their comments. It is Abdullah's hope that this will help the reader to understand a little more about himself. Emotional men will undoubtedly dissociate themselves from many of the cryptic remarks of Zaid, but strangely enough emotional men frequently have less love than moving and intellectual men. Abdul, who had been a hippie, had learned much more about tolerance by living intimately with others, than Zaid, and consequently was more capable of love towards the ignorant Muslims, forgiving much of the stupidity that in the end made Zaid sick physically. The main thing that upset Abdul was being talked down to by well meaning bigots; however, Abdullah explained to him that the upset was only coming from his ego. This idea we have of ourselves is the most vulnerable chink in our armour. Vanity, pride, and self-conceit must always have adulation to thrive on, thus they are the easiest ruffled. Abdullah explained to both Zaid and Abdul that nothing addressed to the body or ego could hurt the spirit, advising them to try to divorce the body and ego from their idea of the spirit, or what they called "I" in themselves.

Neil, Abdul and Zaid had all been upset at the actions of the police in Afghanistan, but certain knowledge gained in Pakistan indicated that the police had some grounds on which to be suspicious. Their fears were unfounded, as can be seen from this book.

By leaving Abdullah shortly after the fast was finished, Zaid missed a great deal of inner work which Abdul was able to experience both with Shaikh Abdul and also Abdullah. Missing the Hajj was regrettable, as it would have given Zaid much to work on. However he was given plenty during the fast, learning a lot about himself in the process.

Because he had the tenacity, Abdul made greater spiritual progress on this journey than Zaid, although Zaid at the inception was more spiritually developed than Abdul. Abdul's impressions of the fast and the Hajj are fairly objective, although many of his questions were of a formatory nature. The impressions of both men were written several months after the fast, while the questions were asked during the actual time of the fast. A comparison of these will enable the reader to gauge the spiritual growth of each man. Neither of them had seen the epilogue written by Abdullah in New Zealand, because Zaid was in England, Abdul in Germany. As can be seen by Abdul's account, many assertions made by Abdullah were confirmed.

Ramdas's Anandashram

Zaid: We were made welcome and at home and cared for in a most sincere way. Our needs were considered in every small detail. The instrument of most of this consideration was Venkatachalam, who became a friend. The time was a restful one, physically, mentally and spiritually. Knowledge was gained; the whole pattern of life at the ashram was a practical working example of Bhakti Yoga. Devotion, particularly on the part of the women, was demonstrated again and again. Experience of the regular daily prayers and songs was most valuable. One result of this participation was a feeling of affinity with all the other people at the ashram, similar to the love for a family. The melodies used for the Ram mantram and the atmosphere in which it was repeated had the effect of fixing it firmly in the consciousness.

During the talks that Neil had with Swami Satchitananda it was apparent that this man listened with both assent and interest to Neil's expression of his own views. At one time the Swami seemed to want to learn from Neil, particularly about the use of the pendulum.

Abdul: Basically the attitude I adopted throughout my stay at the ashram with Abdullah (Neil) and Zaid (Denis) was one of wait and see. Essentially, I suppose, this is the Abdul part of me, because the Christopher Robin part was only too ready to come up with some off-the-cuff opinions which later, on further reflection, were either modified or cancelled out. The Abdul attitude was that I didn't have any readily attainable guideline within myself to really *see* what was going on in the ashram and, for that matter, going on in myself. I was impressed at one level by the obvious peace of Mother Krishnabai and Swami Satchitananda. Despite the fact that Mataji was obviously quite ill, she nevertheless always radiated a feeling of calm—self-possessedness—which never seemed to cease, whether she was carrying out the rituals of the temple, directing the workers who came to her windows for instructions, or talking with Abdullah via Swamiji.

The whole ashram radiated this feeling of calm. In part it could be said to be a play on one's imagination of the setting of the ashram on a gentle tree-clad slope up which a soft cooling breeze always seemed to be moving. In part it was the people with whom one associated in the temple, who were outwardly always calm and quiet. This in itself contrasted with the heavy feeling one got from the poverty and human degradation of the surrounding villages and their inhabitants. In part the calm seemed to be what I thought of as an essence part of the ashram coming from the work of Ramdas on himself and those around him, and having continuity to this moment. Abdullah's comments about Mataji still being attached to the life of the ashram — directing people and being the king-pin of life there — I found very useful, because it explained to a degree the obvious complete involvement of the devotees at the ashram with Mataji and the Swamiji.

However, I could not, at the present stage of development at any rate, have spent very much more time than I did at the ashram. I began to see how easy it would be to slip into a simple, unthinking ritual existence, without the jolts and shocks which I find a vital part of Gurdjieff's and Abdullah's teaching. The ashram was too passive for me, maybe at the level of Christopher Robin, but nevertheless this was a strong feeling inside me, which would make it impossible for me to continue work at this level.

With Abdullah's help, and inner pondering, I was

able to get from the six days we spent at Anandashram an idea of the meaning of service and devotion without seeking reward. Also, experiencing the Om Sri Ram Jai Ram Jai Jai Ram mantram of Ramdas in its own setting added a useful tool for dealing with the inner gabble.

Abdullah and Neil found no surprise in the comments of Denis and Zaid, and Chris and Abdul. Their reactions to the ashram were equal to their spiritual development. The important factor was that both became aware of the mantram and absorbed some of the peace. Bhakti Yoga is attractive to emotional man; in this case Zaid is seen to be an emotional man and Abdul an intellectual man. As Abdul was fighting the "hippy" part of himself, he was aware of the danger of his laziness in the ashram life. Zaid would see that ashram life would give him plenty of scope to work against imagination.

Sanyas Ashram

Zaid: At first view, this place did not measure up to our fixed ideas of what an ashram should be like. The low buildings and high walls forming a large, bare compound like an arena in which the sun blistered down on the combatants in the round of daily existence; the treelessness — no shade except that cast by the buildings; the semi-desert landscape reflected in the bare concrete walls and floors of the cells in which we kept our possessions; the total absence of any furniture on which to sit or lie; all of these things indicated a Spartan life that was harsher than we had expected.

We soon found, in the person of Muniji Maharaj, a warmth and consideration for our spiritual and physical needs which contrasted with the apparent unfriendliness of the environment in which he chose to conduct his work.

From the moment we were welcomed, and continuing throughout our four-day stay, there was a sense of fun and jollity conveyed by Muniji and the other all-male members of his small community. It was also clear to us, on that first day, that the Maharaj is a man of powerful perception and highly balanced development.

Although he had taken a vow of silence Muniji was quick to convey to us, by pointing to passages in the Gita and other writings, pertinent references to our shortcomings and to our inner state. It was not possible to hide anything from this man. He seemed to be aware and in control of everything going on inside the ashram and the people.

Apart from the handful of men and boys residing in the ashram many local professional men are also his pupils and, at some time, have done their stint as "chelas" living within the walls. A number of these men are now teachers working in the town schools and coming each evening to see their guru.

The relationship between Neil and Muniji was one of brotherhood and equality. Although Muniji quizzed Neil intensively about the merit of a 40-day fast he accepted Neil's reasons and was most concerned at all times about his well-being.

We accepted and even welcomed the mild hardships of our stay at Sanyas Ashram because we realised that it was a valuable time of learning and experience which required just those unaccustomed conditions to generate. Apart from personal impressions, the most significant thing seemed to be the part that Muniji Maharaj played in shaping the course of the critical part of the first octave of Neil's fast, by his insistence that we travel only on the eighth day. This guidance was followed, and our transition to Delhi was accomplished in the way that was meant to be.

Abdul: From the soft sea breezes of Ramdas's Anandashram to the oven-heat austerity of Muniji's Shri Dutta Mandir Sanyas Ashram was a big climatic leap and it was all too easy to allow one's psychological state to be ruled by the 40° C. + temperatures which beat out of a brassy Rajasthan sky from 9 a.m. till 4.30 p.m. The heat cut you down in your tracks. None of the usual distractions of going off for a walk into town, reading a book, writing a letter, having a sleep etc. had much appeal because whatever you did, wherever you were, the heat hammered its way into your consciousness. In such surroundings the body was no longer particularly aroused by the thought of food — rather, a seat under the "cold" water tap in the central compound took on much more significance. The austerity of the environment was matched by the man Muniji himself. Gaunt of frame and clad usually only in a worn, saffron-coloured dhoti and a casually wrapped head turban, he passed silently through all the activities of the ashram giving constant guidance and attention — an all-seeing eye conveying very much the traditional idea of the guru I had imagined at home in New Zealand. Yet with all his seeming severity I found him to be a man of real warmth who could still smile at the contradictions of life and who appeared full of compassion for his fellow men — a compassion which was demonstrated again and again in his concern over Abdullah's health and his solicitousness over our food and personal comfort.

I felt at home at Muniji's ashram, and explain this as being due in part to the much more active, masculine nature of Muniji and his teachings and the pervading sense of brotherhood amongst his disciples.

Abdullah's fast

Zaid: Outwardly and physically the fast appeared to be less strenuous than was expected. Circumstances (Allah) seemed to throw many obstacles in Abdullah's way to make conditions more difficult. Various forms of temptation were offered to induce Abdullah to break or modify the fast. The fast was accomplished by means of a faith and a power of will that we do not possess and do not fully understand.

On the ninth day of the forty, at Sarai Rohila railway station near Delhi, it was noticed that Abdullah's eyes had a clarity and intensity of gaze that would be described by the subjective witness as "startling". The eyes were normally kept half-closed, but on this occasion, with Abdullah sitting inside a stationary train and Zaid observing from the platform, the light behind the eyes was clearly evident. The second experience occurred two days after the end of the fast. When Abdullah placed his hand on Zaid's head to heal the fever, there was a sensation of coloured light.

The subjective witness of the fast was disappointed to find no apparent miraculous transformation at the end.

Abdul: It's hard to face the fact that your normal daily round is performed in a sleeping state, particularly when your hopes and prayers lie elsewhere, but despite the daily exposure to the pressures of the spiritual life my regular response to events during our journey was completely dictated by the reflexive, unconscious attitudes and reactions to inner and outer events nurtured in New Zealand.

As the fast proceeded, with its continuous shocks to those around Abdullah, what did happen was that I became a little more aware that in this alien country, in contact with a vital spiritual experience, the body, the ego, the old destructive habits of a past life still piped and danced to their own tune. I'd catch myself dodging a camel caravan in a dusty Kandahar backstreet with as much awareness of the dimensions of my new scale of life as a sleepwalker rising from his bed. When it became possible to hold onto a state of awareness, then for that moment, as long as it lasted, it became possible to see the surrounding world as it really was — not a somehow distorted piece of hometown New Zealand. Some people may learn their life lessons easily. I became sadly aware that hammer blows — psychic dynamite explosions — were needed to shift me off the old way of automated responses.

The scale of what Abdullah was doing with the 40-day fast was, of course, apparent on a conscious intellectual level. Indeed, one had only to observe the shocked reaction of our Muslim friends, who found the standard Ramadhan fast testing enough, to realise that a 40-day fast on water alone while also obeying the Ramadhan restrictions against food and drink during daylight, was a very big thing. I had to starve myself for six days to realise what the fast really meant at a body level.

As Zaid and I joined Abdullah in his fast on the last eight days we began to experience, in the only way possible, what work on oneself at this level really means. We could make excuses that repeated attacks of dysentery had lowered our physical fitness, but after four days of being without food, drinking water only at night, I myself was beginning to feel distinctly like a dying man. The front steps up to Shaikh Abdul's room became a minor mountain and our parade through the insane bureaucracy of the Kandahar Police Visa Office on my fourth fasting day, a Gethsemane I'd hate to repeat. But it was the thirty-seventh day for Abdullah and though his steps were as slow as ours, nothing else showed in his manner to suggest that he'd been without food for that period. Physical strength had nothing to do with it. It was more the fact that a developed man at a higher level of being can call on resources that are not available to the normal man. One was reminded that Irish hunger-strikers were bed-ridden and close to death at the stage where Abdullah was still walking the streets of Kandahar and visiting his own teacher, Shaikh Abdul.

By the sixth day of our own fast it took a great physical and mental effort just to walk to the bathroom and I was beginning to look at the fact of a 40-day fast with real awe — an awe which had its seat in a body well and truly awake to what 40 days without food meant. Intellectual concepts, unfortunately, are not sufficient for aware living.

When the guns were fired to announce the end of

Ramadhan and the beginning of the feast of Ede, it became obvious that we would all be under siege from our Muslim friends if a show of eating wasn't put on by Zaid and I to protect Abdullah and his aim of completing the 40 days. No arm-twisting needed there, I'm afraid. After the first food the body quickly reasserted itself, and without the beady eyes of Abdullah I might have made it within a couple of weeks as the Kandahar Fat Man. It's uncanny to look back on this period from a distance of four months as I doubt if ever before or since, even though fasting is no new experience, I've felt so hungry.

The last week, the last octave, of the fast was obviously going to be a trying time for Abdullah. We tried to think of ways he could be more comfortable and suffer less from the phlegm which was causing his painful vomiting, but one had to come back all the time to the realisation that this was a situation deliberately created outside the realms of the "normal" and the "rational" — that the cure was simple and easy like all the remedies of the unconscious life, but that if one wants to transcend the normal mode of existence then one must realise the supreme place of conscious suffering.

Life in Kandahar during the fast had a timeless quality. Days took aeons to pass. India and the beginning of the fast, way back at Ramdas's Anandashram, seemed years in the past. Imprinted on the inner eye from hours of lying on my bed in the golden Kandahar afternoons waiting for time to pass, is a vision of pine trees outside our bedroom — branches etched against the sun. The activities of the Secret Police had screened us from casual visits from our Muslim friends. We'd cut ourselves off from the meals and cups of tea which punctuate a day and provide a distraction. Except for the break provided by the BBC Foreign Service at 5.30 p.m., each one had to rely on his own inner resources. From this period and later events I learned something about patience, something from Abdullah's own mantram, "Allah knows".

Central behind the Four Ways is the idea that man can be changed, can rise beyond the petty restrictions, the time-wasting antics of ordinary life. Muniji Maharaj at the Merta City ashram had called Abdullah a "Mahatma". This respect for Abdullah which we found in the East whenever we met people following the spiritual path, was salutary to observe. Abdullah and his New Zealand group are a tiny fraction of a complacent, materialistic population in cultural isolation in the South Pacific, and it is easy to be assailed by doubts about the teaching in such a spiritual wilderness. In the countries we travelled through we met men and women who had been involved in some process of spiritual development for the greater part of their lives. They were observably "better" people, with a calm which marked them out from their fellows, and they recognised and accepted Abdullah as one of themselves.

After the rigours of the fast and its seemingly interminable progression, I was a little surprised at how matter-of-factly I accepted the passing of Day 40. Long nights in our hotel room, particularly when I had been fasting myself, had made me aware that Abdullah rarely slept except for relatively brief periods. But the soundness of his sleep on the last night of the fast was unusual enough to be noticed. From Abdullah's own account of what occurred during this sound sleep I became aware again that a man's spiritual progress is not measured by spectacular events occurring in the public eye. Unlike phoney gurus who plague the West with their spurious claims, the true teacher has no need of display.

It was salutary to observe Shaikh Abdul in this respect. Even though a protracted illness was slowly dragging him down, he had a presence and bearing which clearly separated him from the normal man. His glance was calm and unwavering and his words few, so that his pupils and the people who came, often from a great distance, to get his advice, always listened with rapt attention. Abdullah was his pupil, but not an ordinary pupil, as the Shaikh from time to time in our many meetings made quite clear. "We have in common someone very close to Allah", he remarked after warmly greeting Abdullah at one of our early meetings.

Shaikh Abdul was particularly concerned to hear from Abdullah himself the outcome of the fast, and a week after the fortieth day, when Abdullah was once again eating regularly, we went to a special feast at the Masudi household over which the Shaikh presided. Through Zahman Masudi, Abdullah told Shaikh Abdul that he had continued his fast beyond the end of Ramadhan because he had been told inside himself that this was what he must do. Shaikh Abdul said such an austere fast was against the Shariah of the Prophet. The ordinary man, he said, was not allowed to do this, but Abdullah was not an ordinary man and "obviously you have a very special place in Allah's heart".

Abdullah went on to describe how he had seen the small lights which, according to Naqshibandi teaching, are a guiding sign to the acquisition of what Gurdjieff termed the mental body, but that instead of seeing the Great Light which the Naqshibandis mention, he had fallen into a great sleep from which he had been wakened by Allah calling "Abdullah! Abdullah!" Shaikh Abdul remarked that at the time Abdullah was in his dead sleep he was actually absorbed into Allah, and again emphasised the special place that he must occupy.

It was absorbing to hear the two in conversation, particularly as it confirmed the fact that Abdullah was a special category of teacher who could speak with particular authority — something Ziaul Masheikh Ibrahim, Head of the Naqshibandi, had confirmed seven years ago when he gave Abdullah the title of Shaikh of the Order.

Earlier in the week I had become aware of special powers manifesting themselves in Abdullah when he had been examining the spiritual state of Lalmohammed, the Shaikh's son-in-law, who had responded in a profoundly emotional way to Abdullah's probings. Abdullah had for a long time had a capacity to heal and it was instructive to note the subtle changes in this capacity now that Neil was no longer present. Abdullah had often emphasised the karmic and other roles of illness and was sparing in the use of his ability, spending some time trying to explain to the pupils of Shaikh Abdul that the latter's illness had a positive aspect that they must try to understand.

Some of the changes that occurred from this time became more definable to me as we recommenced our journey towards Arabia and Mecca. Echoes of the old Neil were there from time to time, but Abdullah had a calm and acceptance of whatever happened which I found instructive to observe. It will be obvious that this detachment was tested to the full. The singular stupidity of the Afghani authorities in their treatment of us in Kabul when, for no reason we were ever notified of, we were ordered to get out of the country within two days, was trying enough in itself but was to be part of a recurring pattern of trial and frustration as we moved out of Afghanistan through Pakistan into Arabia.

Afghanistan

Zaid: The experiences on which these notes are based occurred three months ago, and the taste has been tempered by time and reflection.

The initial impression of Afghanistan was of an extremely alien, backward country with a population which seemed to be incredibly childish and stupid. Added to this was the narrowness, bigotry and pedantry of their brand of Muslim religion.

With few exceptions, most contacts with Afghanis gave rise to frustration and contempt. The rare exceptions were displays of warm friendship on the part of a few sincere individuals.

As a people who once possessed great potential because of the cultural and religious influences crossing all their borders, they appear to have failed. Pride and egotism would perhaps be among the causes.

Afghanistan as a place and a part of our Holy Mother the Earth is stark, wild and magnificent. Most of the landscape is just as it was thousands of years ago.

Looking back on the Afghani situation with less emotional reaction, it can be seen that the people are pathetic in their poverty and ignorance. They are currently victims of a military dictatorship, and they are envious of, and bewildered by the greater wealth of their neighbours in Iran and Pakistan.

This strange country has been a crossroads to the great movements of military power in Asia throughout the ages. The role of Afghanistan in the late twentieth century may very well be that of one of the pawns in an even greater power struggle.

The Hajj

Abdul: Only someone who has travelled in the East can attest to the special difficulties of travel for a European in this area. The classic scent of Araby is stale urine, not that of myrrh or sweet incense. The heat, the dirt, the flies, the pervasive lack of any sense of hygiene make living with often gruesome diseases just part of the common daily round, and each meal a game of Russian roulette with dysentery; these trying details become magnified tenfold when coupled with the manic irrationality and incompetence of the standard governmental bureaucrats whose sole function, when not openly touting for the interminable "baksheesh", seems to be to frustrate, annoy, and delay.

Our journey from Afghanistan to Mecca was not just an ordinary journey however, and events continually underlined this. The truth of Shaikh Abdul's statement that Abdullah had a very special place in the heart of Allah was something I became very clearly aware of as time passed. The significance of the excep-

tional help given by Mohammad Yafei at the Saudi
Arabian Embassy in Kabul where we received our
visas and special papers for travel to Mecca, became
apparent only as we arrived in Arabia and saw the
restrictions which the ordinary pilgrim had to face as
to when and how he could move and where he could
stay. Repeatedly, the letter he had so carefully
prepared cleared away problems which could have
seriously delayed us in our pilgrimage. Similarly, the
introduction which Ziaul Masheikh Ibrahim had given
us to Hajji Ali Mohammad in Karachi proved to be a
vital link in the chain of events which culminated in
our arrival at the Bayt-al-Haram in Mecca. Other
events stand out as special marks of the manner in
which Abdullah was cared for, one of which deserves
mention as from it I learned something about the way
Allah works.

Our plane was approaching Medina when Abdullah
was approached by a middle-aged man who suggested
that we should stay with the Tabliah Jumat at the
Masjid El Noor while in Medina, and gave Abdullah
the name and address of the Shaikh who headed the
brotherhood. I was not attracted by the thought of
staying with the brotherhood, on the basis of our experience of them in New Delhi. The tendency of Islamic
dogmaticians to earbash one on the most irrelevant
issues of Faith (such as: which hand one should hold a
teacup in; and where the right foot should be placed in
prayer) was one of the harder things to bear I'd found
already, and I was only too aware of what living with
the Tabliah Jumat, whose appointed task seems often
to be the emphasis of the irrelevant, would be like.

On arrival at Medina I thus took steps to see if alternative accommodation could be arranged and was
given the name of a pilgrim's boarding house. After being given a ride into town by a morose Arab and being
dumped unceremoniously outside what turned out to
be a pretty rough doss-house, we made the best of
things and settled for a cell on the third floor. The
Arabs running the place were an unsavoury-looking

crew with the gold teeth which seem to mark the Arab spiv, and I felt in my bones that another attempted rip-off of the "ferangi" was not too far distant, but slept well nonetheless till the amplified morning call to prayer echoed out from the Prophet's mosque.

Mian Shafi of Karachi had already given Abdullah the name of an old Arabic teacher friend who was supposedly teaching at Medina University and whom he recommended as someone who might be able to help us with our accommodation problem. Abdullah elected to stay behind and watch our baggage while I tried to track down the teacher whose name I paid only casual attention to. Eventually my enquiries led me to the University itself, which is situated some three or four miles from town out in the open desert. I asked some students where the teacher might be. "Oh, he's no longer here. He's become the Shaikh in charge of the Tabliah Jumat Centre at the Masjid El Noor". The wheel had come full circle. I was suitably chastened. "Allah knows!"

Another event which demonstrates this special care occurred just after we'd been dropped off in the middle of Mecca by our Medina taxidriver in the small hours of the morning. We had been fasting already for two days and on top of this I'd spent hours that day chasing through the labyrinthine Arab bureaucracy in Medina trying to get official permission for our taxi journey — a necessity, as we'd already been turned back once. The driver had been asked to deposit us at the Al Fihr Masjid but took little trouble to find where it was, and we found ourselves in a strange town with only the vague directions in Arabic of a woman we'd woken in a neighbouring mosque to tell us where Al Fihr might be. On top of this problem was the fact that Abdullah wished to make the ritual circumnambulations of the Ka'aba required of all Hajjis on arrival, and to do this we would have to find a place of safekeeping for our luggage. The streets were empty and silent. Then a man appeared from out of the shadows — clearly motivated to help us. He told us where the mosque was and helped us carry our baggage to its gate. Then he disappeared as mysteriously as he had come.

Although I would not have described most of the stages of our journey through the East as easy or comfortable, I found the pilgrimage to the Holy Cities of Arabia by far the most taxing. It was only towards the end of the actual Hajj that I began to realise that what Allah was doing was forcing us to face the conclusive fact that Islam was just another religion captured by the Law of Seven; that the Ka'aba and the Prophet's Tomb and even the Shatan stones had become objects of ritual worship; and that the only lively reform movement in Islam — represented by the Tabliah Jumat fellowship — not only ignored the possibility of an inner spiritual teaching in the Koran, but actively campaigned against the very idea that there might be, with a rigid literalism which might have done justice to a society of jurists.

While in Arabia I was interested to discover that people from Bokhara, an ancient Sufi centre where Gurdjieff's own teacher is reputed to have lived, had migrated to Mecca after the Soviet regime had clamped down on religious freedom. I made tentative enquiries in Mecca as to whether any "known Sufis" existed, but the question was scorned as not worthy of a true Muslim, and it became clear that the prejudice against the possibility of a mystical interpretation of the Prophet's teachings which we had already discovered in the Islamic reform movement, was probably anathema to a large number of Arab Muslims also.

A Sufi in Mecca would, at all events, have to play the part of a very sly man. Rampant commercialism of the most spiritually destructive kind was widespread in Mecca to the extent that the Holy of Holies of all Islam, the Ka'aba, was but an adjunct to the main motive for the modern survival of the city — the systematic removal of every last cent a pilgrim might have brought with him. It was typical of the attitude of the Meccan Arabs to the Bayt-al-Haram (Haram Sharief) that when the new building was constructed a large shopping centre was incorporated in its structure. The only thing that could be said for the Meccan merchants was that their greed was if anything "bettered" by their colleagues in Medina, who sent their children into the precincts of the Prophet's last resting place itself in order to tout their wares — to the extent that the main courtyard of the mosque often looked like a marketplace rather than a place of worship.

Trenchant Muslim critics of the Hajj seem to be few and far between, perhaps because fear is such a strong force in Islam as it is practised. We found plenty of degrading spectacles to warrant comment. Men fought for places in the front prayer rows of the Prophet's mosque in Medina, caring little if they forced out of place men who had been sitting there for four hours or more. The shoving, punching and kicking that went on wherever "two or three are gathered together in My Name" was a consistent feature of the Hajj and nothing was done to control it by the Saudi authorities, with the odd ineffectual exception.

The culminating riot, for it could be called little else, took place around the Shatan stones in Mina, several miles outside Mecca where I, for all my size and weight, was knocked to the ground and had my watch removed by a band of Central Africans who bludgeoned all before them in an insensate forced passage through the packed crowd. Twenty people were trampled to death that day, we were told, and the report was easy to believe. Certainly no nation in the throng would have taken honours in politeness except the South-East Asian Muslims whose small size and good manners made them easy victims of the crushing crowds. It was not surprising to discover that the Indonesian Government had warned the Saudis that unless measures were taken to police the crowd during the next Hajj season, they would not be allowing any of their own nationals over the age of 40 to travel to Arabia.

Ideally, the pilgrim sleeps at least three nights in Mina but after the first night we were in little mood to continue the punishment. The Mina streets ran with urine, and the diarrhoeic turds which lay everywhere, due to the almost complete lack of any toilet facilities, gave the lie to the proud Arab boast that *they* never suffered from dysentery. The only public toilets, for some classic Arab reason, were locked at night and, at any rate, although newly built, were a squalid uncleaned mess giving point to the blunt British phrase to describe incompetence: "They couldn't even run a public shit house!" To cap it all, fresh water taps were few and far between, and invariably had a heaving scrum around them.

We returned to our sleeping place on the roof of the mosque I was already calling "Hellfire". On the second day of the Shatan stoning we journeyed out to Mina, more as observers than anything else. I had begun to come to terms with the fact that there was a much bigger thing behind this pilgrimage of ours than I had earlier thought, that related directly to the course which Abdullah's teaching would take in the future. Personally, I knew I had to be bludgeoned between the eyes in order to learn something, and the Hajj was the blunt instrument to teach me the crucial lesson of Islam which I might never have learned for some time, had I not embarked on it. I learned that a dead religion can take a long time to decompose. The stench of its rotting was most penetrating at the slaughtering grounds outside Mina where hundreds of thousands of animals, from sheep and goats to camels, are ritually slaughtered in commemoration of Abraham's original sacrifice. In the Prophet's time the sacrificial flesh was used to feed the poor, but Mohammed could never have forseen the day when two million Muslim fundamentalists would follow in his footsteps. What I saw made me angry and disgusted at man's stupidity. I could understand something of the mentality behind the flashing knives of the peasant folk in the blood-lusting crowd, but what contortions of rationalisation were going on in the minds of the more informed Muslims who were part of the twentieth century, to explain the anarchy that reigned all around us? My two companions, one a well-educated Egyptian, seemed quite at a loss to understand why one should object to the gushing blood, squirming and gasping animals, and the dehumanised people participating in the whole macabre carnival. In the central compound, where the largest (qurbaanee) animals are slaughtered, carcase was being butchered on top of carcase. Bulging entrails, shit and blood squelched everywhere underfoot, and I began to feel the gulf which separates this insane expression of religious fanaticism from the subtle workings of the Spirit. No wonder so few Muslims we met could grasp the inner meaning behind their religion, if a display such as this could leave them still contented.

As I left the grounds, workmen were throwing ammonium chloride onto heaps of carcases shovelled together by bulldozers from the previous day's carnage. It could have been symbolic.

"O Ye who believe! The idolaters only are unclean. So let them not come near the Inviolable Place of Worship after this their year. If ye fear poverty (from the loss of their merchandise) Allah shall preserve you of His bounty if He will. Lo! Allah is Knower, Wise."
(Surah 9, v.28, Koran, Pickthall trans.)

Postscript

In reference to Abdul's remarks about Islam dying, Abdullah would like to say that all organised religions must come under the Law of Seven in their outer manifestations. The inner parts of all religions usually say the same truth. As a Sufi, Abdullah believes people must find this inner truth for themselves, from within the framework of whatever religion they happen to belong to. He sees the religion of the future to be cosmic in character, practised by people on their own, not relying on large gatherings at mosques, synagogues, temples, or churches. Until that time, he prays people will try to cultivate some tolerance and understanding of all religions. There are services of Ba'hai and Universal Worship of Hazrat Inayat Khan which cultivate this ideal for those who require outer worship of this calibre. Those who are firmly entrenched in the Buddhist, Muslim, Christian, or other religions must try and see the others' point of view if they are not capable of realising that interiorly all are the same.

The greatest problem of all organised religions is the slavish attitude to the profit motive. Whether governments are avowed capitalists as the U.S.A., socialist as the U.K., or communist as Russia and China, all are dominated by the profit motive. Churches in these countries usually advocate rewards and punishments, clinging tightly to their possessions whilst trying to justify their investments. Many people will say there are no churches in Russia and

China, but Abdullah believes the State is the church and the ideology of communism the religion of these places.

In New Zealand recently there was a great furore over a woman using the allegedly obscene word "bullshit" in a public place; around the same time a television news programme reported how the E.E.C. was embarrassed by the quantity of skim milk powder in their stores, and had the temerity to show how it had to be de-humanised to allow it to be fed to animals. Could there be anything more obscene than this kissing the whip that scourges? All this is done in the name of the profit motive. New Zealand has made a point of avoiding sporting contact with South Africa, as a protest against apartheid, but recently our Prime Minister confirmed that it does not stop us from trading with South Africa. In this morning's paper is an article advocating the "life-boat technique" in dealing with such countries as India, Bangladesh, and certain very depressed African states; however, without the profit motive the world could support millions more people. The food obscenely wasted by those living in well-developed countries would sustain millions of people in under-developed countries. A million or so dollars of Saudi Arabian oil money would provide a modern meat works to enable the sacrificial animals to be prudently used as tinned meat to feed the poor, just as the surplus skim milk from the E.E.C. could feed others. If one were to look at other countries and their surpluses it would be seen that we are propping up an outmoded, horrible profit motive.

As this book bears witness, Abdullah believes in self-discipline, knowing that a person must make the body obedient before much real balanced work can be done on the spirit. In the same way, unless nations can make the profit motive obedient, it is bullshit to talk about aid to this or that country. Ignorance is no excuse in things spiritual or temporal, so it behoves all of us to work to change ourselves, in order to change the inequality in the world today.

To help understand some of the aspects of the fast, Abdullah will endeavour to give the reader a few ideas to work on himself. When a parable is objective, as is the one of the Crucifixion in the Christian Gospels, it has three meanings and seven aspects. Contained in the report of this fast on a literal level are several such stories, used to get the reader to delve a lot deeper than the surface. Abdullah does not intend to elucidate further on this scale, as he knows that for a person to gain real knowledge of this nature he must find these meanings and aspects for himself. If the reader is conversant with the Christian story of the Crucifixion he suggests he or she try to understand the following:

Who are the people on each side of Christ?
Who are the Jews who lusted for his blood?
Who is Pontius Pilate?
What is the significance of the cross?
What other reasons for the 40 days?
Why twelve disciples?
Who was the most conscious actor of the play?
Why did Peter deny him three times?
Who loved him the most?
Why did the soldiers cast lots for the clothes?
Why did he carry the cross?
What do Mary and the other women who loved him so
    much represent?
Why the vinegar and crown of thorns?
Why did he utter the words of despair on the cross?
Who actually is Christ, and what was his real purpose?

The reader must find the answers to these questions from himself if they are to have any real value. Usually when one can formulate a question the answer is contained in it. The correct answer must come from the spirit, not, as many people think, the emotions or intellect.

Salaam Alikoom

New Zealand, India, Afghanistan, Arabia, 1974.
Pakistan and New Zealand, 1975.

Glossary

Allah O Akbar: God is Great.

baraka: helpful vibration coming from teacher.
body kesdjan: vessel of the spirit. Property of a Man No. 4 (G.T.)[1]

centres: (G.T.) Gurdjieff believed man to have three centres or brains. The moving-instinctive-sex centre is situated from the back of the head down the spine to the coccyx; the emotional centre in the solar plexus; the intellectual centre in the head.
conscious shock: self-administered shock. Bridging an interval (G.T.).

darshan: Hindu expression similar in meaning to baraka.

ego: the idea we have of ourselves — usually the body.
ego, destruction of: the aim of Sufis, Gnostics, Hindus and all real teachings. It is only by the destruction of the ego that the pupil can come to a real realization of God.
emotions, negative: e.g. greed, lust, jealousy, etc.
emotions, positive: e.g. acceptance, remorse, love, etc.
external considering: seeing the other person's point of view; assessing, not judging. (G.T.)

formatory apparatus: the shallow memory banks, the frontal brain in the head.(G.T.)
formatory question: one not motivated by genuine personal experience.

goaffadh birds: the experiment in consciousness on the earth previous to man; also called djinns, spirits.
guide to conscience: the mediator between God and man within each person.

[1] Gurdjieff Terminology.

Glossary

Gurdjieff, Georges Ivanovitch, born 1877. The exponent of a system for the harmonious development of man. See his books *Herald of Coming Good; All and Everything; Meetings with Remarkable Men;* and *Life is Real Only Then, When 'I Am'.*

Gurdjieff movements: Temple dances, Dervish dances and a system of graceful posturing with body.

Gurdjieff Work: A name given by pupils to his system.

guru: Hindu name for teacher.

Hazrat Ali: Born 10 years before the Holy Prophet commenced his mission. Fourth Caliph; married Fatima, the Holy Prophet's daughter. He and Khadya, the Holy Prophet's wife, became the first Muslims.

Hazrat Inayat Khan: Sufi teacher who gave out the Message to the West from 1910 until his death in 1927.

Hermes Trismegistus: legendary teacher of Gnostics.

His Endlessness: Gurdjieff's name for the Absolute. The Creator of Everything Existing.

inner considering: indulging in negative emotions such as self pity, resenting. (G.T.)

kundalini shakati: the serpent power or sex energy, raised up through the chakras, centres or lotuses.

Law of Seven: (G.T.) The cyclic law, understood by seven-day week or tonic solfah.

Law of Three: (G.T.) The creative law necessitating a positive, negative and neutralising force.

Lila of God: (Hindu) The play of God.

Lord of our Galaxy: The centre of our galaxy. The giant sun Antares or Ahura Mazda.

magnetic centre: seed of the soul. (G.T.)

Man No.1: (G.T.) Instinctive man.

2:	Emotional man.
3:	Intellectual man.
4:	Balanced man with body kesdjan.
5:	Balanced man with mental body.
6:	Balanced man with beginning of real I.
7:	Perfected man.

mental body: the fourth degree of spiritual growth. (G.T.)

name: the three centres working in harmony in a person instead of only one centre or the body and ego.

name, to make passive: the name is passive to the soul or spirit.

Naqshibandi Order: Sufis belonging to Muslim faith.